JAMES AND
1 & 2 PETER

H. A. IRONSIDE

JAMES AND
1 & 2 PETER

An Ironside Expository Commentary

H. A. Ironside

James and 1 & 2 Peter: An Ironside Expository Commentary

Originally published in 1947. Reprinted in 2008 by Kregel Publications, a division of Kregel Inc., 2450 Oak Industrial Dr., NE, Grand Rapids, MI 49505.

Unless otherwise noted, Scripture quotations are from the King James Version of the Holy Bible.

Scripture quotations marked RV are from the Revised Version of the Holy Bible (Church of England, 1885).

ISBN 978-0-8254-4790-7, print
ISBN 978-0-8254-0268-5, Kindle

Printed in the United States of America

CONTENTS

Part 3: 2 Peter

PART 1

JAMES

INTRODUCTION

It was F. W. Grant, the able and conscientious Bible expositor, whose works have been of inestimable value to unnumbered thousands of God's beloved children, who drew attention, some years before his home-call in 1902, to the fact that in the New Testament we have an epistle written by Jacob to the descendants of Israel! For our English name James is really the equivalent of Jacob (Jacobos in Greek), and is the same as Jacques in French, Iago in Italian, Diego in Spanish, and other forms in many different languages. But the meaning is ever the same—"the supplanter," or "heel-catcher," the "tripper-up." This is what Jacob of old was. "He took his brother by the heel in the womb" (Hos. 12:3), and he was ever crafty and tricky until renewed by divine grace when he became Israel, "a prince with God."

There were two called James, or Jacob, among the twelve apostles who were selected by our Lord on earth: James the son of Zebedee, the brother of John, the beloved disciple, and James the son of Alpheus, brother of Judas, not Iscariot. Apparently neither of these wrote the Epistle we are to consider. Certainly the first did not, for he was slain by Herod very soon after Pentecost. James the

Less, as the other is generally called, has been thought by some to be the writer of this letter. But the greater consensus of opinion credits it to another Jacob altogether—James the brother of our Lord after the flesh.* This is the one who occupied so prominent a place in the Jerusalem church, as mentioned in the book of Acts. He was considered by the early church as a son of Mary and Joseph, born after Jesus came, who is called her first-born. In later years, when the idea of Mary's perpetual virginity began to be promulgated, it was suggested that James was a son of Joseph by a former marriage, and so only a half-brother of our Lord. But the Scriptures appear to negate this idea. See particularly Matthew 12:46–47; 13:55; Mark 3:31–32; Luke 8:19–20; and 1 Corinthians 9:5. All these passages would seem to prove conclusively that Mary had other children besides Jesus. We are told in John 7:5 that these brethren did not believe in the messianic claims of Jesus during the time preceding His resurrection. But after He rose from the dead He appeared to James (1 Cor. 15:7), and as a result of this, undoubtedly, he, whom Paul calls so definitely "James the Lord's brother" (Gal. 1:19), became a devoted follower of Him whom he had not understood before. It is evident from the record in the book of Acts that this man soon became an outstanding leader among the Christians in Jerusalem, so much so that some going from there to the churches founded by Paul are said to have come from James (Gal. 2:12), although he had already disavowed having authorized them to use his name as an endorsement of their legal teaching (Acts 15:24).

The fact that his name is mentioned first in Galatians 2:9—"James, Cephas, and John, who seemed to be pillars"—is significant and indicates the prominent place he held in the church at Jerusalem. We may dismiss, however, as mere unfounded tradition the story handed down from early days that he was consecrated by the apostles as the first bishop of Jerusalem. Nevertheless, he occupied the position of moderator at the council held to determine the attitude of that church toward the missionary work of Paul and Barnabas, as narrated in Acts 15. It was he who summed up the testimony given, and suggested the writing of a letter to assure Christians from among the nations that they were not considered as under obligation to observe Jewish customs.

That James himself was to the last intensely Jewish is evident from the advice he gave Paul when he came to Jerusalem bringing alms for his nation. James

---

* Many think of these two as identical, and there is a bare possibility that such may be the case. Writing on the epistle of Jude many years ago, I expressed myself as fully persuaded of this, but further study has made me feel this position is probably wrong. In my book on Jude [*The Epistles of John and Jude* (Kregel, 2008)], I have allowed the view to stand, which I then held, but would urge the reader to weigh carefully the other view and to accept that which seems to be most reliable.

suggested that Paul should be at charges for some brethren who were about to complete their nazariteship, and Paul was preparing to do this as being made all things to all men so that he might win some, when he was arrested and put in duress.

Many besides Martin Luther have thought that in the letter of James they detected contradictory teaching to that of Paul as set forth in Romans and Galatians. A careful examination of these letters, however, will show that they were treating of altogether different subjects. Paul was dwelling on justification before God, James on justification before men. Had Luther seen this in his early days and put more stress upon it, he might have saved many of his followers from resting on mere credulity instead of knowing the reality of saving faith.

It is not possible to decide with any certainty just when the epistle of James was written. Many have supposed it was the earliest New Testament book, designed to bridge the gulf between the Old and New Dispensations, and so to prepare the way for Paul's gospel, which was to follow. In so writing I do not mean to intimate that Paul preached a different gospel to that of the other apostles, for this he, himself, vehemently denies in Galatians 1:6–9. But the risen Lord gave to him a fuller understanding of the results of the work of Christ than had been revealed previously. Paul alone speaks of justification from all things, rather than mere forgiveness, precious as that is.

It is quite possible that James wrote very shortly after Pentecost. Yet his letter presupposes a reasonably full acquaintance with the great truths of Christianity and its diffusion throughout the entire world where the people of Israel were scattered.

Because of this familiarity with Christianity, others have concluded that, instead of being the first inspired message to the twelve tribes in the new age, the epistle may have been written quite late, after several of Paul's epistles were in circulation, notably that to the Romans. In this case the teaching of justification by works in chapter 3 would be designed to correct a misunderstanding bordering on antinomianism on the part of some, who were pushing Paul's teaching to an extreme that he never intended.

The letter was addressed not to any individual church or group of churches, as such, but to the twelve tribes of Israel in the dispersion, those twelve tribes of whom Paul speaks in his address before Agrippa (Acts 26:7). To these James, or Jacob, their own brother after the flesh, wrote, putting before them the claims of Jesus the Lord of glory. The church and the synagogue were not yet fully separated from each other. Many believing Israelites mingled with their Jewish brethren in the synagogue services, where there was considerable liberty permitted for those of diverse views to express themselves. But these considerations should not lead any Christian to ignore or look lightly upon this epistle, for, after all, in the body of Christ all distinctions between Jew and Gentile are done away; and although there were Jewish groups of believers who did not fraternize fully with Gentile Christians, they were one in Christ whether or not they realized it. And all moral and spiritual truth, wherever found, is for us who now believe in the Lord Jesus Christ and own Him as our Head.

The theme of the epistle is "A Living Faith," a faith that is evidenced by righteous living and godly behavior.

The five chapters seem to present five divisions and may be designated as follows:

Chapter 1: A Victorious Faith
Chapter 2: A Manifested Faith
Chapter 3: A Controlling and Energizing Faith
Chapter 4: A Submissive Faith
Chapter 5: A Patient and Expectant Faith

Throughout the epistle we will recognize a very close connection between its instruction and that given by our Lord in the Sermon on the Mount (Matt. 5–7). It deals not with deep and abstruse doctrinal themes but with practical Christian ethics.

CHAPTER 1

A Victorious Faith

James 1

It is a grave mistake to infer, as some have done, that this epistle emphasizes works rather than faith. It stresses the importance of faith throughout, but shows that real faith is never separated from a life of piety.

In verse 1 we have the salutation. If we are correct in attributing the writing of this epistle to James, the Lord's brother, the way in which he speaks of himself becomes all the more striking: "James, a servant of God and of the Lord Jesus Christ"! If he had known Christ after the flesh, he knew Him so no more. He honors Him as Lord and Messiah, and links His name with that of God the Father. Whatever doubts James may have entertained concerning the claims of Jesus in the days of His flesh, he has none now. All have been dissipated by the resurrection of the One with whom he sustained so intimate a relationship in the Nazareth home.

He writes "to the twelve tribes which are scattered abroad." As a Jew himself, but a Jew who knows the Lord in the fullness of resurrection life, James now speaks to all his brethren in Israel whose fathers had been for centuries dispersed among the nations, and who themselves were scattered far and wide. Many of these knew Jesus as the Christ. If any should read this letter who did not have this knowledge, it was the desire of James to bring them to know Him who is, in Himself, the fulfillment of all Israel's hopes.

It is not for those of us who are Gentile Christians to ignore this portion of Scripture as though, not being Israelites, it had no message for us. But just as the letters written by Paul to Gentile Christians were generally for all believers, whatever their former nationality or relationship, so this epistle contains precious and important truth for the edification and sanctification of all who, like its writer, are slaves of God and of Christ.

In verses 3 to 5 we have an admonition to patience in adversity, which links very intimately with what Paul has written in Romans 5:1–5.

> My brethren, count it all joy when ye fall into divers temptations; knowing this, that the trying of your faith worketh patience. But let patience have her perfect work, that ye may be perfect and entire, wanting nothing. (vv. 2–4)

It is no evidence of God's displeasure when His people are called upon to pass through great trials. If someone professes to have faith in the Lord, he can depend upon it that his profession will be put to the test sooner or later. Alas, that we so frequently lose courage and become despondent in the hour of temptation, instead of realizing that it is the very time when we should look up into the Father's face with confidence, knowing that He is working out some purpose in us that could not be wrought out in any other way. We are called upon to count it all joy when we fall into many trials. The word "temptation," as used here, does not refer to our being tempted to sin, but rather as when God did tempt Abraham, to the testing of our faith. Paul tells us that tribulation worketh patience, and James affirms the same: "The trying of your faith worketh patience." By nature we are inclined to be fretful and impatient. Even Christians sometimes rebel against the ways of God when these go contrary to their own desires. But he who learns to be submissive to whatever God permits glorifies Him who orders all things according to the counsel of His own will.

David said his soul had quieted itself as a weaned child (Ps. 31:2). This is patience exemplified. When natural nourishment is taken from a babe, and it is fed on other food more suitable for its age, it becomes peevish and fretful. But when actually weaned all this is ended, and it accepts gratefully the proffered refreshment.

As we grow in this grace of patience until there is no longer any rebellion against the will of God, a strong Christian character is developed. We become mature and whole, no longer craving for what God sees fit to withhold. This is real victory. To achieve it requires superhuman wisdom, but this God is waiting to bestow in answer to prayer.

> If any of you lack wisdom, let him ask of God, that giveth to all men liberally, and upbraideth not; and it shall be given him. But let him ask in faith, nothing wavering. For he that wavereth is like a wave of the sea driven with the wind and tossed. For let not that man think that he shall receive any thing of the Lord. A double minded man is unstable in all his ways. (vv. 5–8)

It was certainly grace working in his own soul that led James to write this. We all lack wisdom. Yet he does not charge us with our ignorance, but puts us on the ground of possibly needing help from God along this line. "If any of you lack wisdom"! Who does not realize this lack in his own life if at all characterized by the spirit of humility?

But knowing our need is the first step toward receiving that which will meet the need. So we are urged to ask of God—He who is infinite in wisdom, and who delights to give to us according to our need when we come to Him as children to a Father.

It is God's pleasure to give wisdom to those who ask in faith, but if we make request in a formal manner without implicit confidence in His readiness to answer, we only dishonor Him, and so there is no response. To ask in faith necessitates knowing that our petition is in accordance with His will. But we may be assured it is always His desire to impart the necessary wisdom to His people that will enable them to pursue a right course through this scene.

To pray with hesitation or wavering is to fail of blessing. Such an one is as unstable as the waves of the sea driven hither and yon by contrary winds. The man of God is not to be given to change (Prov. 24:21). He who continuously veers from one course to another only reveals his own instability and lack of a sense of being under the divine control. Paul wrote to the Galatians (Gal. 5:8),

"This persuasibleness cometh not of Him that calleth you" (literal rendering). The man who habitually looks to God for guidance will be certain of his path.

A double-minded man is never sure of anything. He goes from one calling to another and from one line of service to another, like a bee or a butterfly flitting from flower to flower, but is ever unsettled and fancies some other course might be better than the one he has taken. "The meek will he guide in judgment: and the meek will he teach his way" (Ps. 25:9). Changeableness is an evidence of an unsubdued will and generally, too, of an inflated ego, which leads one to be occupied unduly with the importance of his own affairs.

> Let the brother of low degree rejoice in that he is exalted: but the rich, in that he is made low: because as the flower of the grass he shall pass away. For the sun is no sooner risen with a burning heat, but it withereth the grass, and the flower thereof falleth, and the grace of the fashion of it perisheth: so also shall the rich man fade away in his ways. Blessed is the man that endureth temptation: for when he is tried, he shall receive the crown of life, which the Lord hath promised to them that love him. (vv. 9–12)

Lowliness of mind is ever becoming in those who profess to follow Him who said, "I am meek and lowly in heart" (Matt. 11:29). If He gives promotion one can rejoice in His goodness, recognizing it all as pure grace, but if He permits conditions to change so that he who was well-to-do finds himself in comparative poverty, let him accept all as from the hand of Him who makes no mistakes. Man, after all, is but as grass and as the flower of the field; he soon passes from this scene, no matter how high or low his lot may be for the moment. The flower may flourish for a few days and be admired by all who behold it, but the heat of the sun soon withers it, and it fades and falls. Even so men may have their hours of exaltation, reveling in their riches and the privileges that wealth can give, but soon all this must come to an end; and unless they possess eternal riches laid up in heaven they will be utterly bereft.

Verse 12 has in view the tried and tested believer who is assured of blessing as he endures grief for Christ's sake. When the temptation is over and he has remained steadfast to the end, he is promised the crown of life, which the Lord will bestow upon all who have shown by their devotion to Him that they truly loved Him. This is not to be confounded with eternal life, which is the free gift of God, the portion of all who believe in the Lord Jesus Christ. The crown of life is reward for faithful endurance out of love for the Savior. It is the martyr's crown, as we see in Revelation 2:10: "Be thou faithful unto death, and I will give thee a crown of life."

Eternal life can never be forfeited. It is the common life of all the redeemed. Those who possess it shall never perish (John 10:25–29). But the crown of life may be lost, yea, will be lost if one should prove recreant to the trust committed to him. So we are warned, "Hold that fast which thou hast, that no man take thy crown" (Rev. 3:11).

> Let no man say when he is tempted, I am tempted of God: for God cannot be tempted with evil, neither tempteth He any man: but every man is tempted, when he is drawn away of his own lust, and enticed. Then when lust hath conceived, it bringeth forth sin: and sin, when it is finished, bringeth forth death. Do not err, my beloved brethren. (vv. 13–16)

James has spoken of temptation in the sense of testing, or trial. Now he turns to speak of it as incitement to sin. It is never right to attribute such temptation to the infinitely Holy One, our God, who has called us to holiness of life. He cannot be tempted with evil; it is ever abhorrent to Him. Neither does He ever tempt anyone. Rather by many means does He seek to induce us to flee from temptation and to take the path of holy subjection to His will.

Jesus taught His disciples to pray, "Lead us not into temptation." That is, Do not leave us to go our own dangerous way, which would expose us to grievous pressure from the enemy of our souls, which, in a moment of weakness, might cause us to fall into great sin, even as David did when he dilly-dallied at home instead of leading Israel to battle against their enemies.

We are tempted, not by God, but by the strength of our own lustful desires. We, being deceived by the craving for self-gratification, are ever in danger of yielding to temptation if we do not reckon ourselves dead indeed unto sin but alive unto God, as Paul tells us in Romans 6.

Lust dwelt upon brings forth positive sin, for as a man thinketh in his heart so is he (Prov. 23:7). Sin indulged in leads to death, for "the soul that sinneth, it shall die" (Ezek. 18:4).

It is the principle James is establishing here, even as in Romans 8:6 we read, "to be carnally minded [or, the minding of the flesh] is death." We need to be careful that we make no mistake as to this. It is never safe to trifle with sin.

> Every good gift and every perfect gift is from above, and cometh down from the Father of lights, with whom is no variableness, neither shadow of turning. Of his own will begat he us with the word of truth, that we should be a kind of firstfruits of his creatures. Wherefore, my beloved brethren,

let every man be swift to hear, slow to speak, slow to wrath: for the wrath of man worketh not the righteousness of God. Wherefore lay apart all filthiness and superfluity of naughtiness, and receive with meekness the engrafted word, which is able to save your souls. (vv. 17–21)

The grateful heart receives all as from God, knowing that every good and perfect gift (everything that He gives answers to this description) comes down from heaven, from the Father of lights. He knows what is in the darkness, but the light dwells with Him (Dan. 2:22), with whom is neither changeableness nor shadow cast by turning. Every blessing for time and eternity we owe to the unfailing goodness and unalterable purpose of grace.

Our new birth itself was the expression of His good will. He brought the Word of truth to bear upon our consciences, leading us to confess our sins and trust the Savior He provided. So we became a new offering of firstfruits, the pledge of the great harvest to be reaped in due time. Christ Himself, in His resurrection, is called the firstfruits of them that slept, and all His redeemed in the present age of grace make up the complete presentation of the new creation offering, prior to the vast millennial ingathering.

As the objects of such matchless grace it surely becomes us to be careful to represent aright the One to whom we owe so much. Therefore we are exhorted as beloved brethren to be quick to hear and heed the Word, slow to express ourselves, unless instructed by the Spirit of God. And above all, slow to wrath, or indignation, let the provocation be what it may; for our anger leading to attempting to repay our adversaries in kind is never in accord with the righteousness of God. This expression is not used here as by Paul in Romans and elsewhere. It does not have to do with that righteousness in which the justified soul stands before God, but rather the righteous character of God, which leads Him to deal with sin according to its deserts.

It behooves us, therefore, as those born of God, to judge in ourselves every tendency to uncleanness or abundance of evil (of which our natural hearts are full), and to receive in simplicity the inwrought Word of God through which we find practical deliverance from the unholy tendencies with which we find ourselves in conflict. The salvation of the soul here is not our redemption from the judgment our sins deserve, but it refers to the purification of our affections, which are the expression of our soul's activities.

But be ye doers of the word, and not hearers only, deceiving your own selves. For if any be a hearer of the word, and not a doer, he is like unto a man beholding his natural face in a glass: for he beholdeth himself, and goeth his way, and straightway forgetteth what manner of man he was. But whoso looketh into the perfect law of liberty, and continueth therein, he being not a forgetful hearer, but a doer of the work, this man shall be blessed in his deed. (vv. 22–25)

Having been born again by the Word, as Peter also tells us (1 Peter 1:23), we are called upon to walk in obedience to the faith as revealed in the Holy Scriptures, not simply hearing what is there written, but making that Word the man of our counsel. To do otherwise is but to be self-deceived, imagining that an intellectual acquaintance with the truths of the Bible is all that is required.

To hear and know the will of God while not obeying it is to be like one looking at his own countenance in a mirror and then going away and forgetting his actual appearance. The Word of God is such a mirror. It was designed to show us what we are, and it thus gives us to see our need of practical cleansing.

This Word is called here the "law of liberty," for it sets forth the principles of behavior in which the newborn man revels. He delights to do the will of God. It is not, therefore, a ministry of condemnation, as was the law to the unregenerate Israelite, but it is a rule of freedom. For he who truly knows the Lord rejoices in His service. He is therefore not merely a hearer but a doer of the Word, and finds blessing in the path of obedience.

If any man among you seem to be religious, and bridleth not his tongue, but deceiveth his own heart, this man's religion is vain. Pure religion and undefiled before God and the Father is this, To visit the fatherless and widows in their affliction, and to keep himself unspotted from the world. (vv. 26–27)

The word *religion* is found only five times in the New Testament, and *religious* but twice. In addition to the instances recorded here, we find Paul using *religion* three times (Acts 26:5; Gal. 1:13–14), and Luke uses the word *religious* once (Acts 13:43). Our English word *religion* comes from the Latin and means, literally, "to bind back," that is, to rebind man to God. As commonly used, it means a system of faith and practice. Three different Greek words are thus translated, one being practically synonymous with our rendering, but when Paul speaks of the Jews' religion he really says "Judaism," and it should have been so rendered. Then when Luke speaks of "religious proselytes" he used a word meaning worshipful adherents.

In these verses James uses the word *threskia*, referring to religious faith, forms, and ceremonies. To be punctilious about these while failing to bridle the tongue, thus guarding against intemperate or unwise speech, is but to deceive oneself. Such religion is mere, empty pretense.

The true religion—or practice of piety—before God and the Father is this: to manifest real concern for the needy, such as orphans and widows, and to walk in holy separation from all uncleanness, thus keeping one's garments unspotted from the world. It is this victorious faith that James insists upon—a faith that enables one to overcome the world and to rise above its sinful follies.

CHAPTER 2

A MANIFESTED FAITH

James 2

This chapter readily divides into two sections: first, verses 1 to 13, and second, verses 14 to 26. In both parts James stresses the importance of reality in one's attitude toward God and His Word. Recognizing that many of those whom he addresses as belonging by nature to the twelve tribes of Israel had in days gone by trusted in obedience to the law given at Sinai as a ground of acceptance with God, James probes the consciences of such in what we might think of as a roundabout way, in order to show them the folly of ever professing to obtain a righteousness of their own through legal observances. In the second part of this chapter he exposes the error of supposing that a mere recognition of the truthfulness of the great outstanding facts of Christianity is a faith that saves. He who has received Christ in reality will manifest his faith by his works.

Let us note then how adroitly this inspired writer reveals the hidden evil of the natural heart.

My brethren, have not the faith of our Lord Jesus Christ, the Lord of glory, with respect of persons. For if there come unto your assembly a man with a gold ring, in goodly apparel, and there come in also a poor man in vile raiment; and ye have respect to him that weareth the gay clothing, and say unto him, Sit thou here in a good place; and say to the poor, Stand thou there, or sit here under my footstool: are ye not then partial in yourselves, and are become judges of evil thoughts? Hearken, my beloved brethren, Hath not God chosen the poor of this world rich in faith, and heirs of the kingdom which He hath promised to them that love Him? But ye have despised the poor. Do not rich men oppress you, and draw you before the judgment seats? Do not they blaspheme that worthy name by the which ye are called? If ye fulfill the royal law according to the scripture, Thou shalt love thy neighbor as thyself, ye do well: but if ye have respect to persons, ye commit sin, and are convinced of the law as transgressors. For whosoever shall keep the whole law, and *yet* offend in one point, he is guilty of all. For he that said, Do not commit adultery, said also, Do not kill. Now if thou commit no adultery, yet if thou kill, thou art become a transgressor of the law. So speak ye, and so do, as they that shall be judged by the law of liberty. For he shall have judgment without mercy, that hath showed no mercy; and mercy rejoiceth against judgment. (vv. 1–13)

Nothing more clearly indicates the selfishness of the human heart than the way in which we are inclined to today (to use a colloquial term) to the wealthy and cultured, while neglecting or ignoring the poor and ignorant. Against this tendency James speaks out vigorously. It is hateful when found in the world and by those who make no Christian or other religious profession at all. It is far more despicable when seen in the sphere where men and women come together presumably to worship God. In such gatherings there should be no place either for such vulgar favoritism of the rich or contempt for the indigent.

To profess faith in the One who, although the Lord of Glory, became on earth so poor that He had no place to lay His head, and yet to have respect of persons in this way, is most inconsistent. All are alike precious to Him, but the poor are in a very special sense the objects of His love and care.

The word rendered "assembly" in verse 2 is really "synagogue." Those to whom James wrote were not, as we have noticed already, separated from the synagogues of the Jews, but still met with their brethren in these centers where

Moses was read and where instruction was given in the Scriptures, as we are told in Acts 15:21, where this same James was the speaker.

As we read what is here written we can see with the mind's eye the worshipers and adherents gathered in the synagogue. Suddenly there is a commotion as the opening door reveals the portly form of a distinguished and wealthy merchant arrayed in costly garb and wearing a gold ring on his finger. Immediately there is a move in his direction by an attendant, or possibly one of the officials, who ostentatiously conducts the newcomer to a choice pew into which he is ushered with every evidence of respect and appreciation, as though he were actually doing the assembly a favor by attending the service. Again the door is opened and there appears a timid-looking man of the poorest laboring class, who looks diffidently about for a place where he will be hidden from observation and yet be able to hear the prayers and the reading of the Scriptures. At first no one makes a move to accommodate him; then finally someone offers him a footstool or a rear seat, which is accepted with becoming humility on the part of the poverty-stricken brother. Surely God would be displeased at such behavior! It would be a perfect revelation of the state of the hearts of those in attendance. Such partiality would show that the thoughts of those so behaving were evil in that they despised the poor and honored the well-to-do.

Yet all are alike precious to God, and He has chosen the poor of this world, made wealthy by faith, as heirs of His kingdom, in which all who love Him shall have part. To despise these is to dishonor Him who recognized them as His own children.

How often had the rich and opulent led in opposition to the gospel and in oppressing those in less fortunate circumstances, even dragging them before the courts in order to defraud them of what was lawfully theirs. These who trusted in their wealth and gloried in their power and influence were often blasphemers of "that worthy name" by which believers in Christ are called.

Jesus declared the second great commandment is "Thou shalt love thy neighbor as thyself." James designates this the royal law. It sums up man's responsibility to his neighbor. He who fulfils it will love all men and look with contempt on none. Therefore, to have respect to persons, preferring one above another, is to violate the letter and spirit of this sacred precept, and so to commit sin and be convicted of the law as a transgressor.

For such an one to pretend to be righteous before God was sheer folly. The law was violated already and so he had no title to expect blessing on the ground of legal obedience. It is not necessary to break every commandment of the law in order to stand condemned as a criminal in the sight of God. To offend in one point is to be guilty of all. The slightest infringement of the law indicates the self-will and insubjection of the heart. Suspend a man over a precipice by a chain of ten links; how many of these need to snap to plunge him into the abyss below? The breaking of the weakest link shatters the chain, and the man falls to his doom.

The same law that forbade adultery, prohibited murder. One need not be guilty of both to be under judgment. To violate either command marked one out as a transgressor of the law. How hopeless then the efforts of anyone to be justified on the ground of his own obedience!

But that law, so terrible to the sinner, is a law of liberty to the regenerated one, because it commands the very behavior in which the one born of God finds his joy and delight. Let the Christian then be careful that he does not act inconsistently with his profession, for "he shall have judgment without mercy, that hath showed no mercy." Under the divine government men reap as they sow; and with what judgment they judge others, they are judged themselves, but "mercy rejoiceth against judgment." It is not the desire of God to deal harshly with anyone. He is ever ready to forgive and bless where sin is recognized and confessed. As objects of such mercy ourselves we are called upon to show mercy and compassion to others, no matter how lowly their condition may be.

This leads naturally to insistence on the importance of a faith that is manifested by good works, and with this the rest of the chapter deals.

> What doth it profit, my brethren, though a man say he hath faith, and have not works? Can faith save him? If a brother or sister be naked, and destitute of daily food, and one of you say unto them, Depart in peace, be ye warmed and filled; notwithstanding ye give them not those things which are needful to the body; what doth it profit? Even so faith, if it hath not works, is dead, being alone. Yea, a man may say, Thou hast faith, and I have works: show me thy faith without thy works, and I will show thee my faith by my works. Thou believest that there is one God; thou doest well: the devils also believe, and tremble. But wilt thou know, O vain man, that faith without works is dead? Was not Abraham our father justified by works, when he had offered Isaac his son upon the altar? Seest thou how faith wrought with his works, and by works was faith made perfect? And the scripture was fulfilled which saith, Abraham believed God, and it was imputed unto him for righteousness: and he was called the Friend of God. Ye see then how that by works a man is justified, and not by faith only. Likewise also was not Rahab the harlot justified by works, when she had received the messengers, and

had sent them out another way? For as the body without the spirit is dead, so faith without works is dead also. (vv. 14–26)

It seems to be a tendency inherent in most of us to go to extremes in matters of doctrine. This is true in regard to the question of our salvation as well as in other things. Some insist that we are saved by character—that only as we do good works and consistently obey the law of God can we be justified. At the other extreme are those who rest solely upon an historical faith for their acceptance with the Lord, ignoring the need of an inner change, which the Savior described as a new birth, and which is evidenced by a life of practical righteousness.

The Holy Spirit used the apostle Paul in a special way to show the fallacy of the first of these views. He insists that justification before God is never by the deeds of the law but by faith in Christ. James deals with the second error, and makes it plain that the faith that saves is a faith that works, and that no one is justified before God who is not justified practically before men. What profit, he asks, if a man says he has faith and his behavior belies his profession? Is this the kind of faith that saves?

He supposes a case where one of Christ's own is bereft of clothing and proper nourishment. Looking upon him in his distress one speaks comforting but useless words, saying, "Depart in peace, be ye warmed and filled," but gives him nothing either in the way of food or clothing to alleviate his needy condition. What profit is there in mere words unaccompanied by deeds of mercy?

In the same way, he undertakes to show that faith divorced from works is dead, being alone. There is no work of grace in the heart where there are no acts of grace in the life. It was Robertson of Brighton who said, "No man is justified by faith, unless faith has made him just." For faith supposes a living link between the soul and God.

James pictures two men; one says to the other, "Thou hast faith, and I have works: show me thy faith without thy works"—something that cannot be done—"and I will show thee my faith by my works"—the only way one can prove to another that his faith is genuine.

To believe the great facts of revelation is not enough: there must be personal commitment of the soul to Christ. Mere monotheism (belief in one God) is not saving faith. The demons believe that God is one, and shudder as they contemplate the day when they must face Him in the final judgment of the wicked dead and of fallen angels. Such belief has no saving value. Again James repeats the statement, "Faith without works is dead." He then cites two Old Testament illustrations to confirm his thesis. First is the case of Abraham, the father of the faithful. What does Scripture teach concerning him? It shows us that he was justified by works when, in obedience to the command of God, he offered up Isaac his son upon the altar.

But Paul tells us plainly in Romans 4:2, "If Abraham were justified by works, he hath whereof to glory; but not before God." Is there not contradiction here? Was not Luther right in declaring that this letter of James' was not true, inspired Scripture but just "an epistle of straw"? Luther and many others failed to note those words, *not before God.* How was Abraham justified before God? James and Paul agree that it was when "Abraham believed God, and it was imputed unto him for righteousness." But when he went to Mount Moriah and there by faith offered his son upon the altar (Heb. 11:17–19), he was justified by works before *men,* as he made manifest the reality of his profession of confidence in God and His Word.

Thus, says James, the Scripture (found in Gen. 15:6) came to fulfillment in the demonstration of that faith Abraham had so long ago. Remember some forty years elapsed between the patriarch's justification by faith before God and his justification by works before men. We may see in this how true it is that a man is justified by works and not by faith only. In other words, as Paul also tells us, faith works by love; otherwise it is not real faith at all.

In Hebrew 11:31 we are told, "By faith the harlot Rahab perished not with them that believed not, when she received the spies with peace." James says, "Likewise also was not Rahab the harlot justified by works, when she had received the messengers, and sent them out another way?" Her faith in the God of Israel caused her to do all she could for the protection of His servants, and secured for her the place of a wife and mother in Israel, bringing her right into the ancestral line of our Lord Jesus Christ (Matt. 1:5). It was faith alone that gave value to the works of either Abraham or Rahab. In one case we see a father about to sacrifice his son, in the other a woman betraying her country! Had there not been confidence in the living God, both acts would have exposed their perpetrators to severe condemnation.

The conclusion is clear in verse 26: "As the body without the spirit is dead, so faith without works is dead also." Death is the separation of the spirit, the real man, from the body, the temporary tabernacle, even as the preacher tells us in Ecclesiastes 12:7: "Then shalt the dust return to the earth as it was: and the spirit shall return unto God who gave it." That lifeless clay is no more dead than a faith that is not manifested by works of righteousness and deeds of piety.

Were we to lose this second chapter of James, we would lose much indeed. We need just such clear, practical instruction to save us from antinomianism and false confidence.

CHAPTER 3

A CONTROLLING AND ENERGIZING FAITH

James 3

The faith of which James writes is a vital force that enables a man to live triumphantly, even to controlling that unruly member, the tongue, by means of which God is so often dishonored and our fellow men injured. An unbridled tongue is at the bottom of much strife, both in the world and in the church. Those who profess faith in our Lord Jesus Christ, who was sinless in word as in all else, may well ponder the serious admonitions of this "tongue" chapter.

My brethren, be not many masters, knowing that we shall receive the greater condemnation. For in many things we offend all. If any man offend not in word, the same is a perfect man, and able also to bridle the whole body. Behold, we put bits in the horses' mouths, that they may obey us; and we turn about their whole body. Behold also the ships, which though they be so great, and are driven of fierce winds, yet are they turned about with a very small helm, whithersoever the governor listeth. Even so the tongue is a little member, and boasteth great things. Behold, now great a matter a little fire kindleth! (vv. 1–5)

In place of *masters* in verse 1 we might better read *teachers*. To be recognized as an instructor of other people is to be in a place of great responsibility. If the teaching given out be faulty or misleading, no one but God Himself can estimate the harm that may accrue to those who receive it. It is a serious thing indeed to attempt to influence men either for good or for evil. He to whom such a ministry is committed needs to be much before God as to how he fulfills it. Far greater condemnation than that to which his listeners are exposed will be his portion if he fails to teach the truth as God has revealed it in His Word. No man who has not been called by the Lord to this work and gifted by the Holy Spirit in order that he may minister to edification should therefore presume to take the place of a teacher. It is the risen Christ who has given gifts to His church, among which are "pastors and teachers" (Eph. 4:11). It is noticeable that the two are intimately connected. Every true pastor should be able to teach the Word in clearness and power, and every God-endowed teacher should have a pastor's heart; otherwise there is the danger of becoming heady and high-minded, and devoting himself simply to imparting information instead of bringing the truth to bear upon the hearts and consciences of his hearers.

Admittedly, there is no perfection even among the choicest of God's children. In many things we all stumble. If one could be found who was never guilty of a slip of the tongue, who never uttered a faulty expression, nor gave vent to an idle or vain word, he would be a thoroughly mature, well-balanced man—perfect as to his behavior and able to hold in restraint every unholy propensity, for there is no part of the body so difficult to control as the tongue.

Horses are held in with bit and bridle (Ps. 32:9) and so rendered subservient to man, whose strength does not compare with theirs. Great ships are controlled and directed in whatever direction the helmsman wishes, by a very small and apparently insignificant rudder. So the tongue, seemingly so weak in itself, has power to make or break one's life and testimony. Nor can any man control it in his own strength. How many a one has determined never again to utter a hasty or unkind word, only to find that, in a moment of thoughtlessness, his best resolution has been broken by the activity of this unruly member, the tongue, whose power for good or evil is so great.

It is a singular fact that the expressive illustration used in the last part of the fifth verse is often so misquoted as to miss the sense of it entirely. People say, "Behold, how great a fire a little matter kindleth!" But that is a complete perversion of the proverb—for a proverb it is. "Behold," says James, "how great a matter a little fire kindleth!" Quoted correctly, we grasp the meaning and visualize the picture at once. A tiny spark may start a conflagration that results in stupendous loss. An unwise or unkind word may be the beginning of trouble that will go on for years and be the means of unceasing strife and division.

> And the tongue is a fire, a world of iniquity: so is the tongue among our members, that it defileth the whole body, and setteth on fire the course of nature; and it is set on fire of hell. For every kind of beasts, and of birds, and of serpents, and of things in the sea, is tamed, and hath been tamed of mankind: but the tongue can no man tame; it is an unruly evil, full of deadly poison. Therewith bless we God, even the Father; and therewith curse we men, which are made after the similitude of God. Out of the same mouth proceedeth blessing and cursing. My brethren, these things ought not so to be. (vv. 6–10)

This little member, the tongue, is likened to a fire that, though small in the beginning, proves devastatingly ruinous as its results spread far and wide. A word has tremendous power for good or ill.

All species and varieties of birds and beasts, even slimy serpents and creatures of the sea, have been tamed by patient handling and attention. But no man can tame his own tongue. It is an irrepressible rebel, an insubject and wicked malefactor, capable of stirring men to every kind of iniquity, and "full of deadly poison." We speak of a scandal monger as having a serpent tongue, and the simile is in full accordance with the damage such an evil speaker inflicts. The amazing thing is that even after a person has been brought to know the Lord, he still finds he has trouble with his tongue. This is because the believer has two natures: the old, corrupt nature inherited from the first Adam, the head of the old creation; and the new and holy nature received from the Last Adam, the Head of the new creation. Such is the power of the old nature that unless there is constant watchfulness and unceasing identification by faith with Christ in His death to sin, it will manifest itself through the tongue long after other evil propensities have been brought into subjection through the power of the cross as applied to the flesh.

Who has not been shocked at times to hear the best of men and those esteemed as the holiest of saints give vent after years of Christian experience to expressions regarding fellow-workmen that indicated an unsubdued nature? With the same tongue we bless God the Father and curse, or injure, men who are made in the image of God. Thus "out of the same mouth proceedeth blessing and cursing." Surely, such things ought not so to be! When they take place, it evidences a lack of communion with God and shows that the heart is, for the moment at least, unsubdued by divine grace.

In nature we never find such an anomaly. No fountain sends forth pure and brackish water from the same vent. Trees bear according to their kind, for they have but one nature. Fig trees do not produce olives, nor do grapevines bear figs. If some have fancied they have seen evidence that James' reasoning in verse 12 is faulty, and have thought they did find both fresh and salt water proceeding from the same fountain, it was because two different underground streams came to the surface very close together, but each opening poured forth only one kind of water. With the tongue it is, alas, otherwise! The same man speaks well of God and ill of man, and often fails to recognize the incongruity of such behavior.

> Who is a wise man and endued with knowledge among you? Let him show out of a good conversation his works with meekness of wisdom. But if ye have bitter envying and strife in your hearts, glory not, and lie not against the truth. (vv. 13–14)

A wise man is a man of faith, a man subject to and taught of God. Such an one will manifest his true spiritual state by good behavior. His speech will be with meekness of wisdom. This will be when faith is in the ascendancy and the old, corrupt nature is kept in the place of death by the power of the indwelling Spirit of God. Where it is otherwise, one may well be ashamed before God and man. If bitter envying and strife are ruling in the heart, it indicates an unsubdued will and life out of harmony with God. For this there is no reasonable excuse, for abundant provision has been made in order that one may be freed from such bondage.

God waits to bestow all needed wisdom to enable us to rise triumphantly above the evil tendencies of our natural hearts. We shall always fail if we seek to be guided by our own minds or by the wisdom of the flesh.

> This wisdom descendeth not from above, but is earthly, sensual, devilish.
> For where envying and strife is, there is confusion and every evil work.

But the wisdom that is from above is first pure, then peaceable, gentle, and easy to be intreated, full of mercy and good fruits, without partiality, and without hypocrisy. And the fruit of righteousness is sown in peace of them that make peace. (vv. 15–18)

The two wisdoms stand out in vivid contrast: that which is of the earth and that which comes from heaven. The former is of this world and is according to nature—that sinful nature, which is in all men since the fall. It is Satanic in origin because the fruit of disobedience to God was at the beginning. It produces envy and strife, lack of restfulness, and every other unholy work.

In contrast to this we are exhorted to seek the wisdom that comes from heaven, which is found in all its fullness in Christ, who is Himself the Wisdom of God, and who unto us who believe is made wisdom, even sanctification and redemption. This wisdom controlling the heart and mind of the man of faith will keep the tongue from evil and the lips from speaking guile. It is first pure; there is no uncleanness in it. Then peaceable, never stirring up to unholy strife; gentle or courteous, never biting nor sarcastic; easy to be entreated, not harsh and implacable; full of mercy, ever ready to manifest pity and compassion and to extend forgiveness to the repentant offender; full, too, of good works, for a tongue controlled by divine grace can be a mighty instrument for good; without partiality, or rather, not given to wrangling or quarreling over places of prefer-ment, or envious because others have received recognition denied to us; and, above all, or in addition to all, without hypocrisy or dissimulation, absolutely honest, and uttering words that can be depended upon as spoken in truth and soberness.

He who possesses this wisdom is enabled so to control his tongue that he sows not the thistle seed of dissension but that good seed, which produces righ-teousness. He sows in peace, because he is a man of peace—a true child of God, a peacemaker, according to the words of our Lord in Matthew 5:9.

When the tongue is surrendered to Christ and dominated by the Spirit, it becomes one of our most useful members; when it falls under the control of the enemy, it works untold grief and damage.

CHAPTER 4

A Submissive Faith

James 4

Faith is hindered by strife and contention, by prayerlessness and by worldliness. Of these James treats in chapter 4 and shows that submission to the will of God enables one to overcome all these tendencies and so to walk in faith, looking to God for His guidance from day to day.

> From whence come wars and fightings among you? Come they not
> hence, even of your lusts that war in your members? Ye lust, and have
> not: ye kill, and desire to have, and cannot obtain: ye fight and war, yet
> ye have not, because ye ask not. Ye ask and receive not, because ye ask
> amiss, that ye may consume it upon your lusts. (vv. 1–3)

Nothing is sadder than grievous misunderstandings among saints. How often whole churches are in uproar over the self-will of one or two who are quarreling over some question of precedence or of manner of service! Wars and fightings (or, brawlings, as the margin has it) arise from the lusts that war in our members—that is, unrestrained and unlawful desires struggling for fulfillment in our very being.

"Ye lust, and have not." The natural heart is never contented. As brought out so vividly in the book of Ecclesiastes, nothing under the sun can satisfy the heart of the man, who is made for eternity. "Ye [envy], and desire to have." The seemingly better fortune of others, instead of leading us to congratulate our brethren in sincerity because of what it has pleased God to bestow upon them, fills us with envy and jealousy if we are not walking in faith and in the Spirit. Thus comes that unholy restlessness that produces strife and confusion. Like spoiled children we become fretful and quarrelsome; nothing pleases. We are continually looking for something new in order that we may obtain the satisfaction that ever seems to elude us. We try everything else before we go to God, forgetting that He alone can meet our needs. Job's friends falsely accused him of restraining prayer (Job 15:4), but the accusation could justly be brought against us. Our Lord has bidden us ask that we might receive. We have not, because we ask not. How true this is of many of us. While God our Father has vast stores of grace and mercy that He is waiting to bestow upon us, we fail to ask, and so we do not receive. We complain of living on at a "poor dying rate"; but the fault is entirely our own. We do not stir ourselves up to pray unto God. And by this very spirit of prayerlessness we give evidence of the low state into which we have fallen.

When at last we do attempt to avail ourselves of the privilege of prayer, our petitions are so self-centered and so concerned about the gratification of our own desires that God cannot in faithfulness grant our requests. True prayer is not asking God to do what we want, but first of all it is asking Him to enable us to do that which He would have us do. Too often we endeavor by prayer to control God instead of taking the place of submission to His holy will. Thus we ask and receive not; because if God answered by *giving* what we desire, we would but consume it on our lusts, or pleasures. To pray aright there must be a separated life, with God Himself before our souls as the supreme object of our affections.

> Ye adulterers and adulteresses, know ye not that the friendship of the world is enmity with God? Whosoever therefore will be a friend of the world is the enemy of God. Do ye think that the scripture saith in vain, The spirit that dwelleth in us lusteth to envy? (vv. 4–5)

Some manuscripts omit the first term "adulterers" and read, "Ye adulteresses." It is as though the Lord were charging us with being like a wife who has proven herself unfaithful to her husband. It is God Himself, revealed in Christ, to whom we owe our fullest affection and allegiance. Worldliness is spiritual adultery. "The friendship of the world is enmity with God." "The world" refers, of course, not to the material universe, but to that ordered system that has rejected Christ. It consists of men and women under the domination of Satan, who is both the prince and the god of this world. Whosoever attempts to go on with the world in any measure is guilty of disloyalty to Him, whom it has spurned and crucified, and he who determines to be a friend of it constitutes himself an enemy of God.

Many are the warnings in Scripture against this unholy alliance of the children of God with the children of the Devil. Through the history of God's dealings with His people He has always called them to holy separation to Himself. It has ever been the effort of the Devil to break down this wall of separation and to lead the two groups to become so intermingled that all vital testimony for God is destroyed. It is impossible to go on in fellowship with the world and yet to walk in fellowship with God. "Can two walk together, except they be agreed?" (Amos 3:3).

Verse 5 is perhaps a bit obscure as we have it in our Authorized Version. "Do ye think that the scripture speaketh in vain, The spirit that dwelleth in us lusteth to envy?" Some have thought the reference was to a part of Genesis 8:21, "The imagination of man's heart is evil from his youth." But this appears to be very far-fetched. Might we not rather read the verse as a question and an assertion? First, "Do ye think that the scripture speaketh in vain?" That is, can we imagine that the many warnings against worldliness found throughout Scripture are all merely empty phrases? Surely not. The Scripture speaks solemnly and definitely against this evil, and we refuse obedience at our peril. Then the last half of the verse refers to the gracious work of the Holy Spirit rather than to the restless cravings of our human spirits. "The Spirit who dwelleth in us yearns enviously." He is grieved and distressed when we prove unfaithful to the Christ, who has redeemed us, and to the Father, who has blessed us so richly. He yearns over us with a holy envy or jealousy, for our God is a jealous God. He would have us wholly for Himself. A divided allegiance means disaster in our own experience and dishonors Him who rightfully claims us as His own. We may shrink from complete surrender to His will, involving utter separation from the world, but as Augustine said, "God's commandings are God's enablings." What He requests He gives us ability to do.

> But he giveth more grace. Wherefore he saith, God resisteth the proud, but giveth grace unto the humble. Submit yourselves therefore to God. Resist the devil, and he will flee from you. Draw nigh to God, and he will draw nigh to you. Cleanse your hands, ye sinners; and purify your hearts, ye double minded. Be afflicted, and mourn, and weep: let your laughter be turned to mourning, and your joy to heaviness. Humble yourselves in the sight of the Lord, and he shall lift you up. (vv. 6–10)

Elsewhere we are bidden to come boldly to a throne of grace, that we may find grace for seasonable help. That grace is given freely to all who come to God in the spirit of self-judgment, seeking the needed strength to so behave ourselves as to glorify Him. He, whose we are and whom we should ever serve, is ready always to supply the needed strength that we may rise above the allurements of the world. But we must approach His throne in lowliness of spirit, for "God resisteth the proud, but giveth grace unto the lowly," as David witnesses in Psalm 138:6, and Solomon likewise in Proverbs 3:34.

As with repentant hearts we bow in submission to the will of God we obtain the grace needed to triumph over every foe. We need not even fear the great archenemy of God and men, the Devil. We need not run in terror from his assaults or faint in fear when he seeks to overcome us. All we need to do is to stand firmly on the ground of redemption, resisting Satan in the power of faith. Notice how both James and Peter agree in this as they write under the guidance of the overruling Holy Spirit. Here James says, "Resist the devil, and he will flee from you." Peter declares, "Your adversary the devil, as a roaring lion, walketh about, seeking whom he may devour: whom resist steadfast in the faith" (1 Peter 5:8–9). By the use of the Word and in dependence on God in prayer we become impregnable against the assaults of the Evil One. The old saying is true:

> Satan trembles when he sees,
> The weakest saint upon his knees.

In John Bunyan's *Pilgrim's Progress*, it was at "Forgetful Green" where he was taken off-guard that Christian was on the point of being defeated by Apollyon, but when he regained the sword of the Spirit, the foe fled.

Several intensely practical admonitions follow in the next three verses. "Draw nigh to God, and he will draw nigh to you." He never refuses to meet the one who sincerely seeks His face. Surely we can each say with David, "It is good for me to draw near to God" (Ps. 73:28). To fail to avail ourselves of this privilege is to wrong our own souls as well as to dishonor Him who invites us to draw nigh. But if we would thus approach Him we must come with clean hands and pure hearts, for He detests hypocrisy and double-mindedness. We must come, too, with chastened spirits; so we read, "Be afflicted, and mourn, and weep: let your laughter be turned to mourning, and your joy to heaviness."

Far too long have we been careless and unconcerned. The place of repentance and sorrow for our many sins becomes us. God has been dishonored by our levity and worldliness; but as we take the place of confession and self-judgment before Him, He is ready to grant us forgiveness, cleansing, and strength for the conflict before us.

His promise is definite, and He will never retract it. He says, "Humble yourselves in the sight of the Lord, and he shall lift you up." He will not upbraid us for our past failures, for when we judge ourselves we shall not be judged (1 Cor. 11:31).

He is ever ready to reach out the hand of help when we come to the end of ourselves.

> Speak not evil one of another, brethren. He that speaketh evil of his brother, and judgeth his brother, speaketh evil of the law, and judgeth the law: but if thou judge the law, thou art not a doer of the law, but a judge. There is one lawgiver, who is able to save and to destroy: who art thou that judgest another? (vv. 11–12)

If saints are to walk together in mutual respect and fellowship, there must be no indulgence in evil-speaking. So we read, "Speak not evil one of another, brethren." To do so is to reflect on God Himself, who in His infinite love and mercy has received us all and put us into this place of holy fellowship one with another. He is the supreme Lawgiver to whom each one is accountable. If I pass judgment on my brethren I am speaking evil of the law and therefore reflecting upon Him who gave it. Each is to answer for himself before God. I cannot answer for my brother, nor he for me. We are all alike called to be doers of the law—that is, to render obedience to the Word. Evil-speaking is in itself disobedience. So if I indulge in and speak disparagingly of my brother, condemning him for disobedience, I am utterly inconsistent, because I am disobedient also. Each must give account directly to God "who is able to save and to destroy." What right then have I to judge another? Paul's words are apropos here: "Therefore, judge nothing before the time, until the Lord come, who both will bring to light the hidden things of darkness, and will make manifest the counsels of the hearts: and then shall every man have praise of God" (1 Cor. 4:5). Our Lord Jesus Himself has commanded us, saying, "Judge not, that ye be not judged" (Matt. 7:1). How easily we forget such admonitions!

The life of faith is one of daily dependence on the Lord, as emphasized in the closing verses of this chapter.

> Go to now, ye that say, To day or to morrow we will go into such a city, and continue there a year, and buy and sell, and get gain: whereas ye know not what shall be on the morrow. For what is your life? It is even a vapor, that appeareth for a little time, and then vanisheth away. For that ye ought to say, If the Lord will, we shall live, and do this, or that. But now ye rejoice in your boastings: all such rejoicing is evil. Therefore to him that knoweth to do good, and doeth it not, to him it is sin. (vv. 13–17)

Although we know that no man can be sure of even another hour of life, let alone of days, months, and years, yet we make our plans and arrangements as though we were sure of being here for years to come. It is not wrong to do this if all is held as in subjection to the divine will. Manifestly we must look ahead and so seek to order our affairs that we can do what is right and necessary as the time goes by. But we are here warned against making such plans in independence of God. In Proverbs 27:1 we read, "Boast not thyself of tomorrow; for thou knowest not what a day may bring forth." And here we are told, "Ye know not what shall be on the morrow." It would seem hardly necessary to be reminded of this, and yet we forget it so readily.

Our life is but as a breath. It is ours for a little time—at the most a few score years—then it vanishes away. We are the creatures of a day; yet we act as though we were going to be here forever!

God would have us dependent on Him from day to day. In looking forward to the future we should seek to know His will. This involves not merely writing "D.V." (*Deo Volente*, "God willing") when we suggest a date for a certain purpose, but also it implies seeking the mind of God before making any such arrangements at all. All should be subject to His will, and if He be pleased to preserve us in life here on earth. To act otherwise is to take an attitude of independence, which ill becomes those whose existence here may be terminated at any moment. To forget this and to act in pride, rejoicing in our boastings, is to dishonor God. "All such rejoicing is evil."

James brings this section to a close with the serious reminder, "Therefore to him that knoweth to do good, and doeth it not, to him it is sin." Sin is any want of conformity to the will of God. When He makes known that will, our responsibility is to act accordingly. Otherwise we miss the mark and incur the divine displeasure. The more clearly God has revealed His mind and the better we understand it, the greater is our responsibility.

CHAPTER 5

A Patient and Expectant Faith

James 5

The believer in Christ is a stranger and a pilgrim, passing on through a world arrayed in opposition against God. He sees confusion and strife on every hand, all the result of sin and rebellion against the only One, who would have brought peace to this troubled scene had men but been ready to receive Him when He came in lowly guise, proclaiming the near approach of the kingdom of the heavens. Because men refused to accept Him, wars and tumults have prevailed ever since, and factions among men of various callings have embroiled one with another in fierce contentions. The struggle between Capital and Labor is pictured in the first part of the present chapter. Nor will these difficulties ever be settled satisfactorily until the Lord returns again to take His great power and reign. To this glad event faith looks on in patience and expectancy.

Go to now, ye rich men, weep and howl for your miseries that shall come upon you. Your riches are corrupted, and your garments are motheaten. Your gold and silver is cankered; and the rust of them shall be a witness against you, and shall eat your flesh as it were fire. Ye have heaped treasure together for the last days. Behold, the hire of the laborers who have reaped down your fields, which is of you kept back by fraud, crieth: and the cries of them which have reaped are entered into the ears of the Lord of Sabbath. Ye have lived in pleasure on the earth, and been wanton; ye have nourished your hearts, as in a day of slaughter. Ye have condemned and killed the just; and he doth not resist you. Be patient therefore, brethren, unto the coming of the Lord. Behold, the husbandman waiteth for the precious fruit of the earth, and hath long patience for it, until he receive the early and latter rain. Be ye also patient; stablish your hearts: for the coming of the Lord draweth nigh. (vv. 1–8)

"Money," we are told, "answereth all things" (Eccl. 10:19). But no man can be certain that his wealth will abide. It may be swept away in a most unexpected manner. The day comes on apace when those who trusted in their riches will weep and howl in their distress as they face multiplied misery and wretchedness, for "Riches profit not in the day of wrath" (Prov. 11:4). And "he that getteth riches, and not by right, shall leave them in the midst of his days, and at his end shall be a fool" (Jer. 17:11). Those who accumulate wealth by oppressing the poor and under-paying those who are employed by them, will find their riches become corrupted and their costly garments moth eaten. The gold and silver they have stored up will become cankered, and the rust of them will become a witness against them, testifying to the greed and covetousness that led them to lay up vast stores of useless pelf that might have been used to the glory of God in alleviating human misery—or, if the heart had been right, in furthering the work of the kingdom of God.

Significantly we are told, "Ye have heaped together treasure for [or in] the last days." There is surely more than a suggestion here that just such conditions as are described shall prevail to an unusually large extent as the end draws on.

No demagogic labor-leader ever spoke out more strongly against this unfairness to the toilers than James does here, as, inspired by the Holy Spirit, he inveighs against such crass selfishness and cruel callousness concerning the needs of the working-classes. "Behold," he exclaims, "the hire [or wages] of the laborers who have reaped down your fields, which is of you kept back by fraud, crieth: and the cries of them which have reaped are entered into the ears of the Lord of Sabbath," that is, of Jehovah of Hosts. Men may think of God as an uninterested spectator, even if He sees at all the wrongs inflicted by one class upon another. But it is not so: on the contrary, He is deeply concerned about all the injustice and oppression that cause such bitter suffering. As of old, He heard the cries of the slaves in Egypt when they sighed and groaned because of their unfair and wicked treatment by the taskmasters of Pharaoh, so He still takes note of every wrong that the privileged and powerful inflict upon the poor and the downtrodden. "When he maketh inquisition for blood, he remembereth them: he forgetteth not the cry of the humble" (Ps. 9:12).

Sternly James rebukes the selfish pleasure lovers who revel in their luxuries, while those whose toil earned the money thus squandered are living in circumstances of the most distressing character. "Ye have lived in pleasure on the earth and been wanton," he exclaims; for wantonness, which covers every form of lechery and immorality, is ever the natural result of such unfeeling callousness concerning the rights of those in less fortunate circumstances. These selfish pleasure-lovers were just like fed cattle nourished for the day of slaughter. Their doom is certain in the day of the Lord's vengeance.

Their attitude toward the poor is the same in character as that of the world toward the Christ of God: "Ye have condemned and killed the Just One; and He doth not resist you." Had they loved Him they would have loved those for whom He died, but having spurned Him we need not be surprised at their heartless indifference to the woes and griefs of those who, like Him, are despised and contemned.

What, then, is the remedy that James sets forth? What cure is there for all this industrial strife? Does he advocate that Christian workmen should join in association with godless confederations of toilers who know not God? Does he suggest that they should unite together and strike for the proper recognition of their just demands? Not at all, for in this case, as in all others, "the wrath of man worketh not the righteousness of God" (1:20). So James puts before the suffering children of God the blessed hope of the Lord's return. Not until He takes over the reins of government will conditions ever be put right in this poor world. So he writes exhorting to patient endurance unto the coming of the Lord. He uses a little parable to show that Christ Himself is the Man of Patience now while He sits upon the Father's throne. For just as the farmer, having sown the seed, waits in patience for the harvest, knowing there must first be the early and then latter rain ere a good crop can be assured, so our blessed Lord, having commissioned His servants to sow the good seed, waits expectantly at God's right hand until "the precious fruit of the earth" is ready to be garnered. We, too, are exhorted to be patient, with hearts established in grace, looking up in faith as we realize that the very conditions depicted only emphasize that "the coming of the Lord draweth nigh."

As objects of grace ourselves we can well afford to show grace to others, even though they treat us despitefully. So he adds,

> Grudge not one against another, brethren, lest ye be condemned: behold, the judge standeth before the door. Take, my brethren, the prophets, who have spoken in the name of the Lord, for an example of suffering affliction, and of patience. Behold, we count them happy which endure. Ye have heard of the patience of Job, and have seen the end of the Lord; that the Lord is very pitiful, and of tender mercy. But above all things, my brethren, swear not, neither by heaven, neither by the earth, neither by any other oath: but let your yea be yea; and your nay, nay; lest ye fall into condemnation. Is any among you afflicted? let him pray. Is any merry? let him sing psalms. (vv. 9–13)

It is not for us to take judgment into our own hands; we are not to endeavor to repay in kind for the evil that unprincipled and wicked men do to us. If we attempt to revenge ourselves we shall fall under condemnation. The only One who can handle aright matters such as these is the Lord Himself; and as the Judge He stands at the door, waiting for the appointed time when He will deal with all who defy the divine law of love.

If any complain of the difficulty that is involved in patiently enduring such wrongs, James points them to the prophets of God in all ages, who have left us examples of patience and long-suffering while enduring the afflictions heaped upon them by wicked men.

If our trials seem inexplicable as we reflect on the character of God, and we find ourselves questioning how a good God can permit such pain—mental as well as physical anguish as we are called upon to endure—James reminds us of the patriarch Job, who, when distressed beyond measure because of the ills he had to bear, yet endured as seeing Him who is invisible, and cried out, "But he knoweth the way that I take: when he hath tried me, I shall come forth as gold" (Job 23:10). The end of the Lord was seen in him when he bowed in humility of spirit before God, exclaiming, "I repent in dust and ashes" (Job 42:6). Well may we take him as our example, and see too in the Lord's final dealings with His poor, troubled servant, that He "is very pitiful, and of tender mercy." Our real victory is found in that self-abasement that justifies God and condemns ourselves.

It ill becomes poor, frail mortals such as we to make strong asseverations, bound by oaths in which we use the sacred name of God and His heavenly abode, or even the earth He has created. In verse 12 we have an echo of our Savior's words as found in Matthew 5:34–37. Oaths of every kind are forbidden. They not only dishonor God and His creation, but also they are most unbecoming on the lips of those who are but creatures of a day, whose every breath depends, from one moment to another, upon the mercy of the Lord.

So he concludes this section by admonishing the afflicted to seek recourse in prayer, assured that God's ear is ever open to our cry. If any are merry—that is, cheerful of heart—let them sing, not the frivolous, empty songs of the world, however beautiful the melodies to which they are set, but psalms, sacred songs of praise, the expressions of a soul that finds its joy in God.

The next three verses bring before us faith's resource in times of illness.

> Is any sick among you? let him call for the elders of the church; and let them pray over him, anointing him with oil in the name of the Lord: and the prayer of faith shall save the sick, and the Lord shall raise him up; and if he have committed sins, they shall be forgiven him. Confess your faults one to another, and pray one for another that ye may be healed. The effectual fervent prayer of a righteous man availeth much. (vv. 14–16)

This passage has been the subject of considerable controversy, and is admittedly difficult to understand unless we keep in mind the special character of this epistle as a last message to the twelve tribes, as such, before the complete separation of Christianity from Judaism, which the epistle to the Hebrews insists upon. God, in condescending grace, meets people where they are, and this is a case in point.

When the twelve apostles went forth to the lost sheep of the house of Israel, they anointed the sick with oil, and God granted healing in response to their faith (Mark 6:13). This is the only other instance in the New Testament where this method is said to have been employed. It is significant because of its definite connection to the testimony to Israel. There may be some truth in the view some have held that the oil was in itself a healing ointment, and that God blessed the means used in connection with the recovery of those who were ill. But James specifically declares, "The prayer of faith shall save the sick," though this would not necessarily mean that any virtue residing in the oil itself was ignored, as God often blesses the means used when prayer also is answered.

The sick were to call for the elders of the church, or the assembly. In the present, broken condition of things in the church it might be difficult to say just where these are to be found. In the beginning it was a simple matter. Elders were appointed in every church, either by direct apostolic authority or by apostolic delegates, as in the instances of Timothy and Titus. It seems that where this special oversight was not available, assemblies appointed their own elders in accordance with the instructions given in the Pastoral Epistles. With no direct apostolic authority today this is all that can be done, and is acted upon in many places. But are these recognized brethren actually elders of the church? One does not want to raise needless questions, but in the endeavor to carry out literally the instruction given here in a day of ruin, they need to be faced honestly.

Throughout Scripture oil is the type or symbol of the Holy Spirit; and in connection with prayer for the sick it would have a beautiful significance. But whether or not any feel free to use it in this way now, it is always right for godly elder brethren to meet with the sick for prayer, and it is just as true now—as in the beginning of the dispensation—that God answers the prayer of faith.

In the case brought before us here it seems to be taken for granted that the illness is part of divine chastening because of sins committed. Therefore when the sick one called for the elders it would in itself be his acknowledgment of his failure. It is not said, however, as Rome would have us believe, that he confessed his sins to the elders: he confessed to God, and if to man also (as in the next verse), it was not as recognizing any special sacerdotal authority on the part of the elders.

It is important also to observe that two very different Greek words are used for *sick* in this verse. "Is any sick among you?" Here the word means "ill," as with some disease. But where we read, "The prayer of faith shall save the sick," the word means "weak," or "exhausted." It might refer to mental depression such as often accompanies illness, particularly when the sick one is conscious that he is afflicted because of his own sins and indiscretions.

"If he have committed sins, they shall be forgiven him." This has to do with the government of God in His own family (see 1 Peter 1:17). The Father judges according to the behavior of His children. When in answer to the prayer of faith the depression of spirit is relieved and the sick one raised up, he may have the assurance of governmental and restorative forgiveness.

In the early days of what is now generally known as "the Brethren Movement," Mr. J. N. Darby and Mr. J. G. Bellett were called in to many sick rooms in

Dublin, where they acted literally upon the directions given here. Many remarkable healings were vouchsafed in answer to the prayer of faith—so much so that attention began to be centered upon these two brethren as special instruments used of God, and in a way that so troubled them, they felt it wise to desist from going, but prayed together or separately for the afflicted in a more private way, acting rather on verse 16 than on verses 14 and 15. God answered in the same grace as when the formal service was carried out.

This is ever faith's resource. Burdened hearts can and should confess their sins one to another when conscious that their illness is chastening for wrong done against the Lord. Then we can pray one for another that healing may ensue: for the earnest prayer of a righteous man is ever effective.

A Roman priest pointed to this Scripture when insisting that it taught confession to one of his order. His hearer responded, "I will confess my sins to you if you will confess yours to me." He refused to recognize the mutual confession here enjoined. There is nothing official or priestly about it.

Then again, there is no authority here for the Romanist "sacrament of extreme unction," which consists in anointing with consecrated oil a person who is about to die. But in these verses the anointing is in view of the sick man's coming back to health, not preparation for death. So readily do Roman apologists seize on the most unlikely passages to bolster up their unscriptural practices and superstitious theories!

Having spoken of the effectiveness of fervent prayer, James introduces the case of Elijah as an illuminating example of what is meant.

> Elias was a man subject to like passions as we are, and he prayed earnestly
> that it might not rain: and it rained not on the earth by the space of
> three years and six months. And he prayed again, and the heaven gave
> rain, and the earth brought forth her fruit. (vv. 17–18)

We are apt to think of prophets and other servants of God mentioned in Holy Writ as men who were of a different fiber than we are, but they were all of the same family of frail humanity, men of like passions with us, but men who dared to believe God and to give Him full control of their lives. In answer to Elijah's earnest prayer, there was not rain in the land of Israel for three-and-a-half years, until godless Ahab was brought to utter despair. Then when the prophet prayed at Carmel, there was "a sound of abundance of rain," bringing gladness to the hearts of men and refreshment to the parched earth. Comment is needless. The story points its own moral.

The epistle closes rather abruptly, as we might think, with a word of encouragement for any who might be used of God to help restore an erring brother.

> Brethren, if any of you do err from the truth, and one convert him; let him know, that he which converteth the sinner from the error of his way shall save a soul from death, and shall hide a multitude of sins. (vv. 19–20)

The sinning one here, as in verse 15 above, is a believer who has gone astray from the path of subjection to the truth. To patiently go after such an one and to convert, or turn, him again to obedience to the Lord is to save a soul from death—physical death, which is the last act of God in His government of His family—and to cover or hide a multitude of sins. This is to practice that charity that Peter also tells us "shall cover the multitude of sins" (1 Peter 4:8), not our own sins of course, but those of the erring brother. By leading him to repentance, so that he judges himself and acknowledges his waywardness, he is restored to fellowship with God and preserved from going deeper into sin, so that the heavy hand of the Lord should have to be upon him in further chastening, even to shortening his life on earth as an evidence of the divine displeasure. This is the same as sinning unto death in 1 John 5:16–17. Many a child of God, because of willfulness and insubjection of spirit, has been taken home far earlier than he would otherwise have been.

In closing our study of this most practical epistle, let us emphasize anew the great importance of a faith that works—a faith that is evidenced by a life of devotion to the Lord, and of concern for the welfare of our brethren in Christ particularly, as well as for all men generally.

PART 2

1 PETER

INTRODUCTION

Epistles of Peter were written primarily—in accord with his special ministry to the circumcision (Gal. 2:8)—to Christian Jews of the dispersion, who dwelt in various provinces in western Asia, where most of the apostle's labors had been. They have to do with the believer's relation to the kingdom of God rather than to the church as the body of Christ; though, of course, those to whom he wrote were, as are all Christians, members of the church and subjects of the kingdom. Both are Wilderness Epistles; they contemplate the children of God, not in their heavenly aspect, as in Ephesians (1:3; 2:6), but rather as strangers and pilgrims journeying on through the wilderness of this world from the cross to the Glory. Peter tells us that he wrote the first letter to testify that "this is the true grace of God wherein ye stand" (1 Peter 5:12). It is not so much the grace that saves (as in Rom. 5:1–2), which gives us a perfect standing before the throne of God; it is rather the grace ministered to us day by day, which enables us to stand against all the wiles of the Enemy and despite all the trials of the way. Suffering has a large place in the epistle. It is looked upon as the normal thing for the believer while pressing on to the inheritance laid up for him in heaven. In this we are reminded of Savonarola's words, "A Christian's life consists in doing good and suffering evil." He is to rejoice for the privilege of suffering for Him, who has redeemed us with His own blood.

The mystery of suffering has perplexed many all down through the ages. It is part of man's sad inheritance because of sin's having come into the world, and in this life the child of God is not exempt from pain, sorrow, and anguish. But the suffering of believers is all ordained of God to work out for blessing. Through this ministry of suffering we are enabled to understand better what our Lord went through for us, when in this scene. He was "a man of sorrows, and acquainted with grief" (Isa. 53:3). God uses suffering to keep us from sin (1 Peter 4:1; 2 Cor. 12:7) and as a means of chastening and discipline (Heb. 12:6–11) whereby we are made more like our blessed Lord. As we suffer because of faithfulness to His name and devotion to His cause, we enjoy a very real sense of fellowship with Him, who is still hated by the world that rejects His testimony. The reward is sure and will make us forget all our light affliction in the enjoyment of the eternal weight of glory (2 Cor. 4:17).

Christians are not exempt from suffering. When a person trusts in Christ, it does not mean that he is at once freed from all the consequences of sin. So far as divine judgment is concerned, he is forever delivered from that (John 3:18 RV); but he is still in the body from which the Adamic curse has not yet been lifted. Consequently, he suffers with the groaning creation, of which that body is still a part. Then, in addition to this, he now finds that the world to which he once belonged has now become a scene of hostility because of the place he has taken in association with a rejected Christ. All this involves suffering, but with every trial and affliction there will come needed grace to endure, "as seeing him who is invisible" (Heb. 11:27).

There is a difference between suffering with Christ (Rom. 8:17) and suffering for Him (Acts 5:41). All Christians suffer with Him because of the very fact that they are partakers of the divine nature, and therefore are quick to feel the adverse conditions through which they are called to pass. But to suffer for Him is to bear shame and reproach—even unto persecution and death—for Christ's name's sake (Acts 9:16).

The apostle Paul tells us in Galatians 2 that after consultation with the leaders at Jerusalem, some time subsequent to his conversion, it was arranged among them that Peter should go especially to the Jews and he to the Gentiles. It was not that either confined himself to one particular class, but He that wrought mightily in Peter to the conversion of the Jews wrought in the same way in Paul to bring the men of the nations to Christ. In his letters, Peter still has particularly in view his brethren after the flesh—the dispersed of Israel—scattered among the nations and living in the countries mentioned in the opening verse of our lesson. These were Jews generally known as the "Diaspora" who, while away from the land of Palestine, yet looked upon it as their native country until they gave up their earthly standing to become members of a new and redeemed nation, whose inheritance was laid up in heaven. To them Peter wrote, encouraging them to trust in the Lord and go on in patience even in the midst of suffering. Of this he had much to say in his letter. It is an epistle for afflicted believers, for, while addressed primarily to Hebrew Christians, it was no more confined to them than Paul's letters addressed to churches among the Gentiles are to be considered as only for those who, by nature, were strangers to the covenant of promise. In Christ there is neither Jew nor Gentile, so what is written to one is intended for the help and instruction of all those who are born again.

First Peter is characteristically a Wilderness Epistle. It pictures believers as journeying on from the place of the blood-sprinkling to the inheritance in heaven, or from the cross to the Glory. Many illustrations are drawn from Israel's journey from Egypt to Canaan. In Ephesians, believers are viewed as already over the Jordan and in the Land, enjoying their inheritance in Christ in the heaven- lies; in 1 Peter, they are seen as a pilgrim people, strangers passing through an unfriendly world, moving on to the Land of Promise.

We are not able to decide exactly when 1 Peter was written, but it was evi- dently well on to the close of Peter's life; and, as he himself connects the two letters so intimately (2 Peter 3:1), they were probably not written very far apart. The date given by Ussher is A.D. 60, but there is no proof that it was as early as that. The best authorities suggest that the first epistle was written somewhere about A.D. 66 or 67, and the second somewhat later. It is evident from 2 Peter 3:15–16 that all of Paul's epistles were in circulation already and recognized as Scripture before Peter wrote this second letter, and we may conclude that the first one was not penned very much earlier.

This first letter readily lends itself to the following outline:

In the Wilderness with God

I. Chapter 1
   A. The trials of the way (vv. 1–12)
   B. Redemption by blood, and new birth by the Word and Spirit of God (vv. 13–25)
II. Chapter 2
   A. A new nation (vv. 1–10)
   B. The pilgrim character (vv. 11–25)

III. Chapter 3
   A. The Christian family (vv. 1–7)
   B. Suffering for righteousness' sake (vv. 8–22)
IV. Chapter 4
   A. The new life contrasted with the old (vv. 1–11)
   B. Suffering as a Christian (vv. 12–19)
V. Chapter 5
   A. The end of the way (vv. 1–4)
   B. Grace operative on the journey (vv. 5–14)

The following is a suggestive outline on the special theme of suffering:

   I. Suffering as a trial of faith (1:6–7)
   II. Christ's predicted sufferings (1:11)
   III. Suffering for conscience' sake (2:19)
   IV. Christ's suffering, our example (2:21–23)
   V. Suffering for righteousness' sake (3:14)
   VI. Christ suffered for our sins (3:18)
   VII. Suffering to cease from sin (4:1)
VIII. Partakers of Christ's sufferings (4:13)
   IX. Suffering as a Christian (4:16)
   X. Suffering for a limited time (5:10)

CHAPTER 1

THE TRIALS OF THE WAY

1 Peter 1

> Peter, an apostle of Jesus Christ, to the strangers scattered throughout
> Pontus, Galatia, Cappadocia, Asia, and Bithynia, elect according to the
> foreknowledge of God the Father, through sanctification of the Spirit,
> unto obedience and sprinkling of the blood of Jesus Christ: Grace unto
> you, and peace, be multiplied. (vv. 1–2)

We have in these opening verses the apostolic salutation. He who had been commissioned by the risen Christ to feed and shepherd the sheep and lambs of His flock addresses himself to those who in years gone by were as sheep without a shepherd, scattered on every high hill, but who now had come under the loving care of the Great Shepherd, who appointed under-shepherds to minister to their peculiar needs.

Peter addresses his letter, "To the strangers scattered." In accordance with the Lord's instruction, Peter seeks to feed and care for these scattered sheep of the house of Israel, dispersed among the nations. The lands mentioned are all in what we call Asia Minor, north of Palestine and Syria, and south of the Black Sea. In these countries lived many Jews who had been brought to know Christ through the ministries of both Paul and Peter. They had lost their old standing as Israelites in the flesh, part of an elect nation, which, however, had failed so grievously. Now, through infinite grace, they belonged to a new country, all of whom were "elect according to the foreknowledge of God the Father." There is nothing fatalistic or arbitrary about election as taught in the Scriptures. The gospel is to be preached to all, and all who believe it may be assured that they are numbered among the elect. Through the Spirit's sanctification—that is, His separating work—men are awakened and brought to see their need of Christ. When in the obedience of faith they appropriate the privilege of finding shelter beneath the sprinkled blood of Jesus, like the people of Israel on the Passover night in Egypt, who were safe within the houses, protected by the blood of the lamb sprinkled on the doorposts and lintels, they are forever safe from the judgment that their sins deserve. God said, of old, "When I see the blood, I will pass over you" (Exod. 12:13). So today, all who are sheltered by the blood of sprinkling may be assured that they stand where the wrath of God will never reach them.

It was to such as these that Peter wrote, wishing that to them grace and peace might be multiplied. It was not the grace that saves that he had in view, but the grace that keeps; nor was it peace with God of which he wrote, but the peace of God that garrisons the hearts of all who learn to commit their way unto the Lord.

The Trials of the Way

The next section, consisting of verses 3–12, constitutes the introduction to the epistle, and gives us the key to the understanding of all that follows.

> Blessed be the God and Father of our Lord Jesus Christ, which according to his abundant mercy hath begotten us again unto a lively hope by the resurrection of Jesus Christ from the dead, to an inheritance incorruptible, and undefiled, and that fadeth not away, reserved in heaven for you, who are kept by the power of God through faith unto salvation ready to be revealed in the last time. Wherein ye greatly rejoice, though now for a season, if need be, ye are in heaviness through manifold temptations: that the trial of your faith, being much

more precious than of gold that perisheth, though it be tried with fire, might be found unto praise and honor and glory at the appearing of Jesus Christ: whom having not seen, ye love; in whom, though now ye see him not, yet believing, ye rejoice with joy unspeakable and full of glory: receiving the end of your faith, even the salvation of your souls. Of which salvation the prophets have enquired and searched diligently, who prophesied of the grace that should come unto you: searching what, or what manner of time the Spirit of Christ which was in them did signify, when it testified beforehand the sufferings of Christ, and the glory that should follow. Unto whom it was revealed, that not unto themselves, but unto us they did minister the things, which are now reported unto you by them that have preached the gospel unto you with the Holy Ghost sent down from heaven; which things the angels desire to look into. (vv. 3–12)

It is noticeable how closely the words of verse 3 are linked to Ephesians 1:3. Both begin in exactly the same way—by blessing, or extolling the God and Father of our Lord Jesus Christ. But as the passages in the two epistles continue, they unfold altogether different aspects of truth. In Ephesians the believer is seen as seated together in the heavenlies in Christ. This is the New Testament antitype of Canaan, the inheritance that is ours already. On the other hand, Peter shows us the believer as journeying on to Canaan rest, which is at the end of the way. Both aspects are true, and the one never contradicts the other. As to our standing, we are in Christ in the heavenlies; as to our state, we are pilgrims marching on to glory.

Ours is a living hope, in contrast to Israel's dead hope, because of their failure to fulfill the terms of the covenant entered into at Sinai. Our confidence rests not on any ability of our own to carry out certain promises, but is according to the abundant mercy that God has bestowed upon us, and that is assured to us by the resurrection of Jesus Christ from the dead.

We are not seen here as already in the enjoyment of our inheritance, but we are journeying on toward it. It is reserved in heaven for us. Unlike Canaan, it is incorruptible and undefiled, and shall never fade away. Even after Israel entered the land of promise, they defiled it by their idolatry, and it became corrupted because of their gross wickedness, so that eventually they lost it altogether. It is far otherwise with our heavenly inheritance. It is being kept for us, and we are kept for it—"Kept by the power of God through faith unto salvation" in its complete and final sense, which will be revealed in the last time, that is, when we reach the end of the wilderness journey. It is not the salvation of the soul of which he speaks here. That is ours already, as we shall see in verse 9. Salvation in its complete sense includes the redemption of the body.

In view of this blessed hope we are enabled to rejoice even though now for a season, if need be, we are in heaviness of spirit because of the many trials to which we are exposed. There is a "need be" (1:6) for every sorrow that the Christian is called upon to endure. Are we willing to trust the wisdom of God and to allow Him to plan our lives as He sees fit? Faith must be tested, otherwise it could not be verified. So we need not fear when our faith is exposed to trial that it indicates any displeasure on God's part toward us. Rather it indicates His deep interest in and concern for us. For just as gold is tried in the fire in order to separate it from the dross, so faith, which is much more precious than gold that perisheth, must be tested in order that it may be found unto praise and honor and glory at the revelation of Jesus Christ from heaven.

"Precious" is one of Peter's special words. He writes of the precious trial of faith (1 Peter 1:7), the precious living Stone (2:4, 7), precious faith (2 Peter 1:1), and precious promises (1:4). Do we appreciate all these precious things enough to suffer for them if called upon to do so? Are we as ready to suffer for the sake of our blessed Lord as we are to profit by His sufferings on our behalf? Even the philosophic worldling can endure suffering without complaining, but it is only the regenerated one who can glory in tribulation. Just as gold is purified by the fire that consumes the dross, so God uses trial and suffering to separate the believer from those things that hinder fellowship with God and growth in the spiritual life.

Faith endures, we are told elsewhere, "as seeing Him who is invisible" (Heb. 11:27); so although we have never seen our blessed Lord with our mortal eyes, we love Him, and believing in Him we rejoice with unspeakable gladness and exalted joy. The expression "full of glory" is a peculiar idiom suggesting an exaltation beyond our power to express. What rapture fills the heart that is really taken up with the unseen Christ, in whom we have put our confidence, so that even here and now we know we have the salvation of our souls! We know this on the authority of the Word of God.

Of this salvation the prophets of ancient times spoke and wrote; but it was not given to them to know the fullness of grace as it has now been revealed to us. They wrote as the Spirit directed concerning "the sufferings of Christ, and the glory that should follow," but they had no way of knowing the exact time when these things were to be fulfilled; neither could they see the long period (this entire present age) that was to elapse between the cross and the glory of the Redeemer.

It was revealed to them that their message had to do with a future day. What they reported by the Spirit's inspiration is now the basis of our confidence and the first source of information for those who have preached the gospel in our day in the energy of the Holy Spirit, who was sent down from heaven at Pentecost to bear witness to these truths—things that had been hidden even from the angels, and which they now delight to look into. They are learning the wisdom of God in us, as we are told in Ephesians 3:10.

Redemption and New Birth

Just as Israel was redeemed by the blood of the lamb on the night of the Passover in Egypt, and that date became to them the beginning of months, when they were born as a nation, so Peter now asks us to consider the marvelous realities of our redemption and our new birth.

> Wherefore gird up the loins of your mind, be sober, and hope to the end for the grace that is to be brought unto you at the revelation of Jesus Christ; as obedient children, not fashioning yourselves according to the former lusts in your ignorance: but as He which hath called you is holy, so be ye holy in all manner of conversation; because it is written, Be ye holy; for I am holy. And if ye call on the Father, who without respect of persons judgeth according to every man's work, pass the time of your sojourning here in fear: forasmuch as ye know that ye were not redeemed with corruptible things, as silver and gold, from your vain conversation received by tradition from your fathers; but with the precious blood of Christ, as of a lamb without blemish and without spot: who verily was foreordained before the foundation of the world, but was manifest in these last times for you, who by Him do believe in God, that raised Him up from the dead, and gave Him glory; that your faith and hope might be in God. Seeing ye have purified your souls in obeying the truth through the Spirit unto unfeigned love of the brethren, see that ye love one another with a pure heart fervently: being born again, not of corruptible seed, but of incorruptible, by the word of God, which liveth and abideth for ever. For all flesh is as grass, and all the glory of man as the flower of grass. The grass withereth, and the flower thereof falleth away: but the word of the Lord endureth for ever. And this is the word which by the gospel is preached unto you. (vv. 13–25)

God's word to Israel, as given in Exodus 12, was that they were to eat the Passover with their loins girded and their shoes on their feet, ready to begin their journey to the promised land the moment the signal was given to evacuate Egypt. So, here, in addressing these sojourners in a world to which they no longer belonged, Peter bids them gird up the loins of their minds—that is, bring every thought into subjection to the revealed will of God, for we are to have the loins girt about with truth (Eph. 6:14). Sobriety is to characterize such, for it is a serious thing to be called out of this world to live for God in the very scene where once we dishonored His name. The hope is to be the guiding-pillar that leads us on to the end of the journey, which will come when Jesus Christ is revealed from heaven.

No longer are we to conduct ourselves, or fashion our behavior as we once did when, in the days at our blindness and ignorance, we were under the domination of carnal desires. Like the Israelite about whose garments was to run a fringe of blue—the reminder that he was linked up with the God of heaven, and upon which he was to look and remember that he was called to exhibit the heavenly character, for God had said, "Be ye holy; for I am holy"—so we, too, are to manifest holiness in all our words and ways as becomes a heavenly people passing through a world of sin.

Neither carelessness nor indifference becomes those who, through infinite grace, are privileged to call God "Father," but in reverent fear, lest we grieve His heart and reflect discredit upon His name.

We have been redeemed, not like Israel when they paid down the half-shekel of silver—as in Exodus 30:12–15, as a ransom for their souls—or with gold—so often demanded as a ransom by some victorious leader when he dictated terms of peace to a conquered people—but we have been purchased and freed from judgment by the precious blood of Christ, and should no longer be conformed to the empty behavior of the past, which, while in accordance with ancestral customs, was opposed to the ways that glorify God. Christ was the true, unblemished and spotless Paschal Lamb—free from sin or fault of any kind, either inwardly or outwardly. Him God had foreknown before the universe was created, because redemption was no after-thought with Him, hastily arranged to patch up a wrecked world, ruined by man's sin and rebellion against his Creator. All had been foreseen and prepared for beforehand. God had not been outwitted by Satan. It was not, however, until man had been tested fully under various dispensations and proven to be utterly helpless so far as delivering himself is concerned, that the remedy God had provided, the Savior He had foreknown, was manifest. Through Him the Father is now made known in the fullness of His grace, and by Him we believe in God who, after Christ had finished His redemptive work, raised His blessed Son from the dead, and glorified Him by seating Him as Man at His own right hand, that our faith, or confidence, and our hope might be in God—the God of resurrection.

Redemption is a work that was accomplished by Christ Jesus on Calvary, and is, therefore, so far as we are concerned, entirely objective. We could have no part in it except that we committed the sins that made it necessary, unless we had been left to die in our iniquities. But regeneration, or new birth, is subjective. It is a work done in us by the Word and the Spirit of God. Of this Peter next speaks.

A great change has taken place within the hearts of all those who have obeyed the truth through the Spirit. The Word of God has been brought home to their souls in the convicting and convincing energy of the Holy Spirit, thus producing a new life and nature, the characteristic feature of which is love—the love of God shed abroad in our hearts, as Paul tells us, by the Holy Spirit who is given unto us (Rom. 5:5). This produces love for our brethren in Christ, a love that is unselfish and pure, not contaminated by the evil desires of the flesh. For all who thus believe in Christ are born again, not a birth according to the natural order, not of corruptible seed; for "that which is born of the flesh is flesh," as Jesus told Nicodemus (John 3:6). But this new birth is, as we have seen, the result of believing the Word of God, which lives and abides forever. And this Word, we are told in verse 25, is that which is proclaimed by the gospel.

The intervening verse, 24, and the first part of verse 25 are parenthetical and emphasize the contrast between that which is human and that which is divine. Peter quotes Isaiah 40:6, 8, declaring that all flesh is as grass, and all the glory of man as the flower of grass, which appears beautiful and verdant for a brief season, and then is gone forever. For the grass soon withers, and the lovely flowers fade and fall, but the Word of the Lord endures forever.

Theologians may wrangle about the necessity of a new birth by the sovereign act of God whereby the elect are first quickened and then enabled to believe unto salvation, but Scripture is clear that new birth is by means of the Word, which the Spirit of God brings to bear upon the heart and conscience. Apart from this there is no divine life. James also tells us that, "Of His own will begat he us by the word of truth" (James 1:18). Believing the gospel, we become children of God, and are responsible to walk as such, in the place of realized dependence upon the Lord from day to day as we pursue our pilgrim course from the cross to the glory yet to be revealed.

CHAPTER 2

A New Nation

1 Peter 2

Wherefore laying aside all malice, and all guile, and hypocrisies, and envies, and all evil speakings, as newborn babes, desire the sincere milk of the word, that ye may grow thereby: if so be ye have tasted that the Lord is gracious. To whom coming, as unto a living stone, disallowed indeed of men, but chosen of God, and precious, ye also, as lively stones, are built up a spiritual house, an holy priesthood, to offer up spiritual sacrifices, acceptable to God by Jesus Christ. Wherefore also it is contained in the scripture, Behold, I lay in Zion a chief corner stone, elect, precious: and he that believeth on Him shall not be confounded. Unto you therefore which believe He is precious: but unto them which be disobedient, the stone which the builders disallowed, the same is made the head of the corner, a stone of stumbling, and a rock of offence, even to them which stumble at the word, being disobedient:

whereunto also they were appointed. But ye are a chosen generation, a royal priesthood, an holy nation, a peculiar people; that ye should show forth the praises of him who hath called you out of darkness into his marvellous light: which in time past were not a people, but are now the people of God: which had not obtained mercy, but now have obtained mercy. (vv. 1–10)

Just as Israel, who went down into Egypt as a family of seventy souls, emerged from that land of bondage a new nation, under the divine leadership, so now believers in Christ, having been born of God, are constituted a new nation, whose citizenship is in heaven, and who, though living in this world, are not of it, nor to be fashioned according to it. Their habits and motives are of an altogether different order to what once characterized them as walking according to the flesh.

It was this that was symbolically emphasized in the imperative command to put away all leaven out of their houses and to eat only unleavened bread with the bitter herbs and the lamb that had been roasted with fire. We are told in 1 Corinthians 5:7–8 to "purge out therefore the old leaven, that ye may be a new lump, as ye are unleavened. For even Christ our Passover is sacrificed for us: therefore let us keep the feast, not with old leaven, neither with the leaven of malice and wickedness; but with the unleavened bread of sincerity and truth." This is that of which Peter exhorts as this new section opens.

One of our hymns says,

> Lord, since we sing as pilgrims,
> O give us pilgrims' ways;
> Low thoughts of self, befitting
> Proclaimers of Thy praise.
> Oh, make us each more holy,
> In spirit pure and meek,
> More like to heavenly citizens
> As more of heaven we speak.
> —Mary Bowley
> "We're Pilgrims in the Wilderness"

Even so are we admonished to lay "aside all malice, and all guile, and hypocrisies, and envies, and all evil speakings." What a clearing out of the old corrupt leaven is suggested here! How tightly these things cling to us even after we have been saved! With what readiness do we yield to the dictates of the old nature, giving way to unholy feelings, engendering evil humors, and forgetting we are to speak evil of no man. A thorough searching of our hearts for leaven such as these words describe, and burning it in the fire of self-judgment, is most important as we begin the heavenward journey.

In order to obtain strength for the way, we need nourishment, and that of a divine order. So just as newborn babes desire milk, we should thirst for the genuine milk of the Word, the revealed truth of God, that feeding upon it, we may grow *unto salvation,* as the Revised Version adds, not in order to obtain salvation in the sense of deliverance from the guilt of sin, but that salvation that means complete conformity to Christ to which we shall never attain until we see Him as He is. In the meantime, the more we meditate upon the Word the more like Christ we shall become, provided of course we have tasted already that the Lord is gracious. If we do not yet know Him, we have not taken the first step in the pilgrim way.

Peter's two letters were based upon two great events in his life—two high and precious experiences that he was never able to forget. The first epistle links definitely with that confession of Christ as the Son of the living God, which Peter made in the coasts of Caesarea Philippi, when Jesus declared, "Blessed art thou, Simon Barjona: for flesh and blood hath not revealed it unto thee, but my Father which is in heaven. And I say also unto thee, That thou art Peter [a stone], and upon this rock I will build my church; and the gates of hell shall not prevail against it" (Matt. 16:17–18).

The second epistle is linked just as definitely with the glorious vision on the mount of transfiguration, as we shall see when we come to consider it.

Whatever man may think, and however theologians may wrangle about the meaning of the Lord's words to Peter regarding the Rock on which the church is built, there can be no room for doubt as to how Peter himself understood them. He writes, "To whom [referring to the Lord of whose grace he had just spoken] coming, as unto a living stone, disallowed indeed of men, but chosen of God, and precious, ye also as living stones, are built up a spiritual house." The house is the church. The Rock upon which it is built is Christ Himself, the Living Stone. Every believer is also a living stone (made such by grace), built upon Christ and cemented to his fellow-members by the Holy Spirit. So, too, teaches the apostle Paul in the closing verses of Ephesians 2.

> View the vast building; see it rise.
> The work how great; the plan how wise!

Nor can that faith be overthrown
Which rests upon the Living Stone.

But not only are believers viewed as stones built together for an habitation of God through the Spirit, we are also "an holy priesthood, to offer up spiritual sacrifices, acceptable to God by Jesus Christ." How different this from Rome's claim to have authority to appoint a special priesthood who offer material sacrifices as they present a wafer before God and pretend it is changed into the body, blood, soul, and divinity of Jesus Christ, and is again immolated on their altars as a perpetual sacrifice for the sins of the living and the dead. The blasphemy of it all chills one's blood even as we pen the words!

In Israel of old there were three special groups: the priesthood, the Levites, and the warriors. In the church, or assembly of God, all are priests, to go unto God as worshipers; all are Levites, to serve their brethren in holy things; all are soldiers, to fight the good fight of faith. There is no separate priesthood now, no clerical order recognized by God as distinct from and with authority over those who are content to be called and call themselves mere laymen, or the laity.

All believers are a holy priesthood, as we learn in verse 9, a royal priesthood also. We offer up the sacrifice of praise, the fruit of our lips, giving thanks to His name (Heb. 13:15). This was the real sacrifice, even in the days of types and shadows (Jer. 33:11).

Reverting to the Rock foundation, Peter quotes from Isaiah 28:16, where of old God declared, "Behold, I lay in Zion a chief corner stone, elect, precious: and he that believeth on him shall not be confounded." He who in God's eyes is the infinitely precious One is the Elect Stone, the Head of the corner, and the solid Rock upon which the spiritual edifice is built. To those who believe in Him, He is, indeed, not only precious, but also the preciousness; but unto the disobedient He is the rejected Stone whom God nevertheless has made Head of the corner (Ps. 118:22). Disowned by Israel and crucified, God raised Him from the dead and exalted Him to this high place. But despite all the many witnesses to His resurrection there are myriads who refuse to believe. They stumble at the Word because of their disobedience, and to this they are appointed. Do not misunderstand; they were not appointed, or predestined, to be disobedient. God does not so deal with any man. The supralapsarian theologians dishonor His name while imagining they are defending His right when they so teach. But when men are determined to go on in the path of disobedience, God gives them up to strong delusion, thus appointing them to stumble. Believers are a chosen generation, not after the flesh, but after the

Spirit; they constitute a royal priesthood who, like Melchizedek, go out from the presence of God to bless mankind, and magnify the name of the Most High God; they are a holy nation, thus taking the place of that polluted nation that God has, for the time being, disowned. This new nation of pilgrims is now His peculiar people—that is, a people for His own possession, whose high calling it is to show forth His praises who has called them out of the darkness of nature, of sin, and of unbelief, into the marvelous light and liberty of the gospel.

In time past, as Hosea predicted (see 2:23), they were not a people; now they are recognized by God as His own. They who were once *Lo-ruhamah* (not having obtained mercy) now have obtained mercy through faith in Christ Jesus the Lord.

The Pilgrim Character

Dearly beloved, I beseech you as strangers and pilgrims, abstain from fleshly lusts, which war against the soul; having your conversation honest among the Gentiles: that, whereas they speak against you as evildoers, they may by your good works, which they shall behold, glorify God in the day of visitation. Submit yourselves to every ordinance of man for the Lord's sake: whether it be to the king, as supreme; or unto governors, as unto them that are sent by him for the punishment of evildoers, and for the praise of them that do well. For so is the will of God, that with well doing ye may put to silence the ignorance of foolish men: as free, and not using your liberty for a cloak of maliciousness, but as the servants of God. Honor all men. Love the brotherhood. Fear God. Honor the king. Servants, be subject to your masters with all fear; not only to the good and gentle, but also to the froward. For this is thankworthy, if a man for conscience toward God endure grief, suffering wrongfully. For what glory is it, if, when ye be buffeted for your faults, ye shall take it patiently? but if, when ye do well, and suffer for it, ye take it patiently, this is acceptable with God. For even hereunto were ye called: because Christ also suffered for us, leaving us an example, that ye should follow his steps: who did no sin, neither was guile found in his mouth: who, when he was reviled, reviled not again: when he suffered, he threatened not; but committed himself to him that judgeth righteously: who His own self bare our sins in his own body on the tree, that we, being dead to sins, should live unto righteousness: by whose stripes ye were healed. For ye were as sheep going astray; but are now returned unto the Shepherd and Bishop of your souls. (vv. 11–25)

The Spirit of God now gives us important details concerning what should characterize the pilgrim band as they travel on through the wilderness of this world to the Canaan rest that awaits them when they reach the end of the way. Let us notice carefully each verse.

"As strangers and pilgrims" (v. 11). Notice the order. Men often reverse it. But no one is really a pilgrim in this Biblical sense who has not first become a stranger in this world. As such, he is to be careful to avoid contamination with the evil that is all about him. He is to "abstain from fleshly lusts, which war against the soul." Just as Amalek came out and fought against Israel (Exod. 17:8), so these carnal desires would tend to turn the believer aside from the path of devotion to Christ, and so hinder his progress as he journeys on toward that which God has prepared for him (1 Peter 1:3–4).

"They may by your good works . . . glorify God" (v. 11). Just as Daniel's enemies had to confess they could find nothing against him (Dan. 6:4–5) except "concerning the law of his God," which was contrary to their accepted heathen practices, so consistent believers shut the mouths of those who would deride and vilify them, making these very foes of the truth bear testimony to the consistency of their lives.

"Submit yourselves to every ordinance of man for the Lord's sake" (v. 13). As loyal subjects of the State, Christians are to be obedient to the laws passed, even though they may feel that in some instances the laws are unnecessarily arbitrary and even actually unjust. By their submission they honor Him whom they recognize as their Lord and Savior. Whatever form of government may prevail, so long as it is recognized as the constituted authority of the country, we are to be in subjection, whether to a king or by whatever name the supreme executive is known.

"Unto governors . . . for the punishment of evildoers" (v. 14). Human government has been established by God that evil may be checked and righteousness encouraged. The fact that some rulers act contrary to the divine ideal does not absolve the believer from obedience to the powers that be. All human government manifests imperfection, but without its restraints, society would be shipwrecked, and anarchy would prevail. In principle, all constituted authority is intended to prevent crime and encourage honesty and good living.

"With well doing ye may put to silence the ignorance of foolish men" (v. 15). Nothing is a better answer to false and malignant accusations than a godly, upright life against which no charges can be brought truthfully. Samuel is a good example of this (1 Sam. 12:3–4). There have not been wanting evilly disposed men in all ages, who have sought to impugn the motives and malign the conduct of God-fearing people. The best answer to all this is a blameless life, and this involves obedience to law.

"As free, and not using your liberty for a cloak of maliciousness" (v. 16). Christians have been called unto liberty (Gal. 5:13), but this must never be confounded with license to obey the dictates of the flesh. He who makes of his Christian profession a cloak to cover unrighteous behavior is a hypocrite who dishonors the worthy name of the One he professes to serve. Note the vivid contrast here. Those who, through grace, are free from the slavery of sin and free from the principle of legality in Christian service are nevertheless the bondmen of God, purchased with the precious blood of Christ, and so responsible to render glad, loving obedience to His Word. They are not to make their liberty an excuse for fleshly license.

There are four admonitions in verse 17. The third really covers all the rest. He who fears—that is, stands in awe of—God will not dishonor any man, and will love his brethren, and give due recognition to constituted authority. "Honor all men." No man is to be despised. All are among those for whom Christ died. "Love the brotherhood." This refers not to the world in general but to those who have been saved out of the world—those born again into the family of God. "Fear God." Reverence Him whom we now know, not only as Creator, but also as Redeemer. "Honor the king." Show due respect to the head of the government as one set by God in that very place, who is therefore accountable to God for the right exercise of the authority committed to him.

Servants are exhorted to obedience to their own masters, and that "not only to the good and gentle, but also to the froward" (v. 18). It is easy to obey a master who is kindly disposed and considerate. But the grace of God is seen in yielding obedience to those who are harsh and needlessly severe. This verse has added force when we remember that in Peter's day servants were generally slaves. The consistent behavior of Christians in bondage was used of God to lead many of their masters to Christ. Self-vindication is ever to be avoided on the part of the follower of Christ. He is called to imitate his master, who endured uncomplainingly the false accusation of sinners and lived His pure and holy life as under the eye of the Father, content to leave it with Him to justify Him in due time (Isa. 50:5–8). The believer is to be subject to the laws of the land wherein he dwells, and to be a loyal citizen and an obedient servant in his particular calling. Thus by his good behavior he will show the falsity of the charges of malicious men, who would seek to make him out a menace to the State and an enemy of mankind. The early Christians were often so charged, but their consistent lives silenced their accusers.

"This is thankworthy" (v. 19). The real theme of Peter's first letter is the grace of God as manifested to and in the saints (5:12). The word rendered "thankworthy" here is really "grace." It is grace active in the life, enabling one to bear up under false accusations and to suffer in silence when conscious of one's own integrity.

"If, when ye do well, and suffer for it, . . . this is acceptable with God" (v. 20). Anyone can endure reproof when he knows it is deserved. It takes grace to enable one to accept undeserved blame without complaining; but to God it is acceptable, or well-pleasing, for this is to follow Christ's blessed example. "It is hard to be blamed for what you did not do!" So said a troubled young Christian lately. But in this portion of God's Word we are bidden to take our blessed, adorable Lord Himself as our example in this as in all else. He was falsely accused and bitterly persecuted for wrongs He had never done. As He left everything in the Father's hands, so should we. Nature will rebel when we have to say, as He did, "They laid to My charge things that I knew not" (Ps. 35:11). But grace will enable us to triumph and to rejoice when men speak evil of us and persecute us (Matt. 5:11). If we endure patiently, as seeing Him who is invisible (Heb. 11:27), we shall be vindicated in His own way and time, and reward will be sure at His judgment seat (1 Cor. 4:5).

"Christ also suffered for us, leaving us an example" (v. 21). He has trodden the path ahead of us. We are called to follow His steps. The word here rendered "example" suggests a top line in a child's copybook. We are to reproduce Christ in our lives.

"Who did no sin, neither was guile found in his mouth" (v. 22). He was pure outwardly and inwardly, God's unblemished, spotless Lamb, therefore a suitable sacrifice on behalf of sinners, as He would not have been had He Himself been in any way defiled.

"When he was reviled, reviled not again" (v. 23). Jesus endured patiently all the shame and indignities to which wicked men subjected Him. Their evil accusations brought no answers from His holy lips. He left it to the Father to vindicate Him, in His own good time.

"Who his own self bare our sins in his own body on the tree" (v. 24). We dislike being blamed for other people's faults, but He took all our sins upon Himself—bore all the judgment due to us—and so we are healed by His stripes, as depicted in Isaiah 53:5–6. Shall we then live in the sins for which He died? Rather, let us live now "unto righteousness" that He may be glorified in us.

"The Shepherd and Bishop of your souls" (v. 25). Once we were all like straying sheep, but through the grace of God we have been brought to know Christ. He is now our Shepherd, feeding and sustaining us, and our Bishop, or Overseer, guiding and directing us as we pursue our onward way through the wilderness of this world.

Having been saved by Him whom the world rejected, His pilgrim people have no reason to expect better treatment from that world than what was meted out to their Lord. When incarnate Love was here on earth, few received Him and many rejected Him. His followers need not be surprised therefore if their testimony is spurned by the majority and accepted by the minority. The Christian is not to think it strange that he, and that for which he stands, is not highly esteemed by the world. He is here as a light to shine for Christ in a dark scene. When Jesus our Lord returns He will estimate aright all His people have done and suffered for His sake, and He will reward accordingly. In the meantime it is better far to have the approval of the Lord than the approbation of the world that crucified Him.

We may epitomize the conduct that is inculcated in this section of the epistle as follows:

Strangers and Pilgrims

- Purity of life (v. 11)
- Honesty in word and deed (v. 12)
- Subjection to law (vv. 13–15)
- Walking in liberty, not license (v. 16)
- Reverence for God and consideration for men (v. 17)
- Obedience to masters (v. 18); enduring grief (v. 19)
- Patient under false accusations (v. 20)
- Following Christ's footsteps (vv. 21–23)
- Dead to sins and living unto righteousness (v. 24)
- Owning Christ's authority, and under His care (v. 25)

These are the characteristics of the new life that we who are saved have received by our second birth.

CHAPTER 3

THE CHRISTIAN FAMILY

1 Peter 3

Likewise, ye wives, be in subjection to your own husbands; that, if any obey not the word, they also may without the word be won by the conversation of the wives; while they behold your chaste conversation coupled with fear. Whose adorning let it not be that outward adorning of plaiting the hair, and of wearing of gold, or of putting on of apparel; but let it be the hidden man of the heart, in that which is not corruptible, even the ornament of a meek and quiet spirit, which is in the sight of God of great price. For after this manner in the old time the holy women also, who trusted in God, adorned themselves, being in subjection unto their own husbands: even as Sara obeyed Abraham, calling him lord: whose daughters ye are, as long as ye do well, and are not afraid with any amazement. Likewise, ye husbands, dwell with them according to knowledge, giving honor unto the wife, as unto the weaker vessel, and as being heirs together of the grace of life; that your prayers be not hindered. (vv. 1–7)

The new life does not run counter to natural relationships. It is no sign of grace but rather quite the opposite to be without natural affection. So the Holy Spirit now proceeds to admonish wives and husbands as to their attitude each to the other.

There are few experiences more difficult than to be united in marriage to an unbeliever. The Christian young man or young woman should never go voluntarily into such a union. "Be ye not unequally yoked together with unbelievers . . . and what communion hath light with darkness? . . . or what part hath he that believeth with an unbeliever?" (2 Cor. 6:14–15). But where one member of a family already formed is brought to know the Lord while the other remains in the darkness of nature, the most serious misunderstandings and perplexing circumstances are apt to arise. If it be the wife who has been converted, while the husband remains out of Christ, peculiar wisdom and grace will be needed on her part. If she takes a superior attitude toward her unsaved husband she will only stir up his opposition to the truth and render conditions increasingly difficult. She is admonished here to be in subjection to her own husband, manifesting such grace and humility of spirit that even though he resents the Word he may be won without the Word—that is, without the wife saying much to him—by her discreet behavior as he observes the beauty of her Christian character. We say that, "Actions speak louder than words," and this is in accord with the teaching of Scripture. An imperious, dominating woman will drive her husband further from God instead of drawing him to Christ. But a gentle, gracious lady, whose life is characterized by purity and whose adorning is not simply that which is outward but that which is inward, will have great influence over even a godless husband.

Here let me point out that the Scriptures do not forbid a measure of adornment of the person, but rather that the wife should not depend on this to make her pleasing and attractive. A slatternly woman only repels. But one may be tastefully attired and immaculately groomed, and yet spoil everything by a haughty spirit or a bad temper. The ornament of a meek and quiet spirit is in God's sight priceless, and will commend her to her husband, family, and friends.

It was in this way that the holy women of old were adorned who lived in dependence on God and were in subjection to their husbands instead of domineering over them. Sara is cited as a beautiful example of this. When the angel announced that she was to become the mother of Isaac, though at a very advanced age, she wonderingly inquired how it could be when she was old and, she added, "My lord being old also," referring to her husband, Abraham. Those who obey this instruction become manifestly her children morally, and need not be terrified by trying and difficult experiences.

To the husbands there is also a word of serious admonition. Let them give all due honor to the wife, not trying to lord it over her conscience, but recognizing her physical limitations as the weaker vessel; let them be the more considerate, dwelling with her according to knowledge and as being heirs together of the grace of life; and the Spirit adds what is most important: "That your prayers be not hindered." Quarrels and bickering in the home stifle all fellowship in prayer. It means much for the husband and wife to be able to kneel together in hallowed communion and mingle their voices in prayer and intercession.

Suffering for Righteousness' Sake

Finally, be ye all of one mind, having compassion one of another, love as brethren, be pitiful, be courteous: not rendering evil for evil, or railing for railing: but contrariwise blessing; knowing that ye are thereunto called, that ye should inherit a blessing. For he that will love life, and see good days, let him refrain his tongue from evil, and his lips that they speak no guile: let him eschew evil, and do good; let him seek peace, and ensue it. For the eyes of the Lord are over the righteous, and his ears are open unto their prayers: but the face of the Lord is against them that do evil. And who is he that will harm you, if ye be followers of that which is good? But and if ye suffer for righteousness' sake, happy are ye: and be not afraid of their terror, neither be troubled; but sanctify the Lord God in your hearts: and be ready always to give an answer to every man that asketh you a reason of the hope that is in you with meekness and fear: having a good conscience; that, whereas they speak evil of you, as of evil-doers, they may be ashamed that falsely accuse your good conversation in Christ. For it is better, if the will of God be so, that ye suffer for well doing, than for evil doing. For Christ also hath once suffered for sins, the Just for the unjust, that he might bring us to God, being put to death in the flesh, but quickened by the Spirit: by which also he went and preached unto the spirits in prison; which sometime were disobedient, when once the longsuffering of God waited in the days of Noah, while the ark was a preparing, wherein few, that is, eight souls were saved by water. The like figure whereunto even baptism doth also now save us (not the putting away of the filth of the flesh, but the answer of a good conscience toward God,) by the resurrection of Jesus Christ: who is gone into heaven, and is on the right hand of God; angels and authorities and powers being made subject unto him. (vv. 8–22)

Verse 8 begins with the word *finally*, which suggests that what follows is not to be divorced from what has gone before but rather is the natural result of it. Believers generally, not only husbands and wives, now are exhorted to manifest oneness of spirit, sympathetic consideration for each other, with brotherly love, the product of a gracious heart and a lowly mind. Anything like retaliation for injuries is to be sedulously avoided. In place of returning evil for evil and reviling for reviling we are to bless even our worst opponents, for in so doing we ourselves will be doubly blessed.

Peter quotes a part of the thirty-fourth Psalm using verses 12 to 16, but he stops in the middle of the last sentence, and that for a very special reason. The psalmist speaks to all who love life and would enjoy it at its best, bidding them keep the tongue from evil and the lips from speaking guile—that is anything of a dishonest character. He exhorts them to turn from evil and pursue righteousness, to seek peace and pursue it—that is, ever follow after that which is for the good of mankind. And all this is in view of the fact that the all-seeing eyes of Jehovah are upon the righteous, and His ears are open to their prayers: but the face of the Lord is against them that do evil. There Peter stops. When we turn back to the Psalm we find the sentence continues by adding, "To cut off the remembrance of them from the earth." But that will not be in this age. It will have its solemn fulfillment in the coming day of the Lord. So exact and meticulous is Scripture! We might think that it made little difference, but Jesus put a whole dispensation into a comma when He read in the synagogue at Nazareth, "He hath sent me . . . to proclaim the acceptable year of the Lord. And He closed the book" (Luke 4:19–20). The next words are, "And the day of vengeance of our God" (Isa. 61:2); but that will not begin until the day of grace is ended.

No matter how evil men, motivated by Satanic hatred for the gospel, may seek to injure believers, "Who is he that will harm you, if ye be followers of that which is good?" There can no evil happen to the righteous, for, "All things work together for good to them that love God, to them who are the called according to His purpose" (Rom. 8:28). This includes persecution, sickness, financial distress—anything that men think of as evil, but all of which God sanctifies to the good of the subject Christian.

If called upon to suffer for righteousness' sake let it be counted a joyful privilege. There is no need to fear or to live in dread of threatened terror, for God is over all, and none can go beyond that which He permits for our blessing. He who stopped the lions' mouths and protected Daniel, and walked in the furnace with the three Hebrew youths, will ever keep a watchful eye upon His saints, yea, and upon their enemies too, lest they go beyond His permissive will.

Only give God His rightful place in the heart. Let it be separated to Him, and when called to witness before men be ever ready to give an answer to all who inquire concerning the basis of your faith, with becoming lowliness and reverence; being careful to maintain a good conscience so that there will be no truth in their charges if accused of evil behavior by wicked men who give false testimony regarding your upright manner of life in Christ.

Verse 17 declares that it is better—that is, preferable—if it pleases God to allow it, that one suffer for doing the right rather than for doing what is wrong. In this our blessed Lord is our supreme example. He suffered at the hands of evil men who misrepresented Him and bore false witness concerning Him. Then on the cross He suffered once for all for sins—not His own but ours—He the Just, we the unjust, in order that He might bring us to God. And this He has done. We have not yet been brought to heaven, but we who believe in Christ Jesus have been brought to God.

On the cross He was put to death in the flesh, but in God's due time He was made alive by the Holy Spirit in His physical resurrection from the dead. Observe, it is not His human spirit that is here in view. It could not properly be said that He was quickened or made alive in that, for His spirit never died. But after the body and spirit had been separated in death, He was raised again by the Holy Spirit (see Rom. 8:11). In that same Spirit, He, in ages long gone by, preached through Noah to spirits with whom He declared He would strive for more than an hundred and twenty years (Gen. 6:3). Noah was a preacher of righteousness and suffered for righteousness' sake, as we are called to do, and as Jesus did (2 Peter 2:5). So it was "when once the longsuffering of God waited in the days of Noah, while the ark was a preparing," that Christ by the Spirit preached in or by the patriarch. What was the result of this preaching? "Wherein few, that is, eight souls were saved by water." And just as those who entered the ark passed through the flood of judgment to a new earth, so in baptism the obedient believer is saved in symbol. It is not the going into the water that saves but that of which baptism speaks and which a good conscience demands: the resurrection of Jesus Christ from the dead. He who went down into death, who could say, "All thy waves and thy billows are gone over me" (Ps. 42:7), has now emerged in triumph, bringing over to new creation all who trust in Him. He has gone into heaven and sits as the exalted Man on the right hand of God, in token of the Father's full satisfaction in the work of His Son. To Him all angels, authorities, and powers are subject.

CHAPTER 4

THE NEW LIFE CONTRASTED WITH THE OLD

1 Peter 4

Conversion to God involves an inward and an outward change. When born again, one receives a new nature with new desires and new ambitions. The whole behavior is changed from that of a selfish worldling to a devoted follower of the Lord Jesus Christ. The great importance of this is emphasized in the opening verses of this chapter.

> Forasmuch then as Christ hath suffered for us in the flesh, arm yourselves
> likewise with the same mind: for he that hath suffered in the flesh hath
> ceased from sin; that he no longer should live the rest of his time in the
> flesh to the lusts of men, but to the will of God. For the time past of our
> life may suffice us to have wrought the will of the Gentiles, when we

walked in lasciviousness, lusts, excess of wine, revellings, banquetings, and abominable idolatries: wherein they think it strange that ye run not with them to the same excess of riot, speaking evil of you: who shall give account to him that is ready to judge the quick and the dead. For this cause was the gospel preached also to them that are dead, that they might be judged according to men in the flesh, but live according to God in the spirit. But the end of all things is at hand: be ye therefore sober, and watch unto prayer. And above all things have fervent charity among yourselves: for charity shall cover the multitude of sins. Use hospitality one to another without grudging. As every man hath received the gift, even so minister the same one to another, as good stewards of the manifold grace of God. If any man speak, let him speak as the oracles of God; if any man minister, let him do it as of the ability which God giveth: that God in all things may be glorified through Jesus Christ, to whom be praise and dominion for ever and ever. Amen. (vv. 1–11)

With Christ Himself as our example of patience in suffering, how can we, who owe all to Him, do otherwise than arm ourselves with the same mind and so endure as beholding Him by faith? Many times God uses suffering to keep us from going into that which would dishonor Him. And when exposed to severe temptation it is as we suffer in the flesh that we are kept from sin. In this we may see the difference between our Lord's temptations and those that we have to face. He was tempted in all points like as we, apart from sin. He did not have a sinful nature as we do. He was from His birth the Holy One. He could say, "The prince of this world cometh and hath nothing in Me." With us it is otherwise. When Satan attacks from without there is an enemy within, "sin, the flesh," that responds to his appeal, and it is only as we reckon ourselves dead indeed unto sin but alive unto God that we are enabled to mortify the deeds of the body. This means suffering, often of a very severe character. But, we are told, Jesus "suffered being tempted" (Heb. 2:18). So infinitely pure and holy was He that it caused Him intense suffering even to be exposed to Satan's solicitations. He overcame by the Word of God, and the Devil left Him for a season, to return in the hour of His agony as He was bearing our sins upon the cross.

Let us therefore resist every temptation to gratify the flesh, cost what it may, for it is our new responsibility to live no longer in the flesh according to carnal desires, but in the Spirit to the glory of God. A careful consideration of Galatians, chapter 5, will help to make clear what Peter here presents to us as our responsibility to refrain from ways that once characterized us. In their unsaved days these whom he addresses wrought the will of the Gentiles when they fellowshipped with the ungodly in lasciviousness, lusts, excess of wine, revelings, banquetings, and the abominations connected with idolatry. Although their pagan Gentile neighbors were after the flesh, the Jews sought to curry favor with them by participating in these evil things, even as Israel of old failed so grievously at Baal-Peor (Num. 25:1–3). Since Gentile conversion to God, all this was changed. Their former companions could not understand why these Gentiles so suddenly and completely turned from lives of self-indulgence to what seemed to them great abstemiousness and austerity. They who applauded them before now spoke evil of them. But they were to live as those who should give account not to men but to Him who is about to judge the living and the dead when He returns in power. In that day those who despised them for their holy lives would answer to God, too. "For this cause was the gospel preached also to them that are dead, that they might be judged according to men in the flesh, but live according to God in the spirit."

Those who had preceded the converted Gentiles in the path of faith had been obliged to contend with similar conditions. The good news was preached to them who, though now dead, once had to face the ridicule and even persecution of wicked men who had no understanding of spiritual things, and it was revealed to them that even while they had lived as men in this scene and been judged by their fellows as fools and fanatics, they might actually live unto God in spirit. There is no thought or suggestion here of the gospel being carried to men after death as Romanists, Mormons, and others, would have us believe.

Verse 7 shows that the Christian is ever to keep the end in view. He is to live not for the passing moment, but as one who knows that the end of all things—that is, all things of this present order—is at hand. It will be ushered in at the Lord's return—therefore the importance of sobriety and watchfulness unto prayer.

Verse 8 emphasizes that upon which Paul lays so much stress in 1 Corinthians 13, the importance of fervent love among those who are of the pilgrim company. The world hates believers. This is all the more reason why they cling to one another in love, even though they cannot be blind to the faults of others, but love covers the multitude of sins, rather than exposing and holding them up to censure. This does not mean that we should be indifferent to evil. We are taught elsewhere how to deal with and to help those who are overtaken in a fault or who drift into sin. See Galatians 6:1; James 5:19–20.

It is incumbent on those who love Christ to be gracious to one another, using hospitality ungrudgingly, as verse 9 tells us.

Verses 10 and 11 have to do with the exercise of spiritual gifts and Christian service generally. Each is responsible to use the gift he has received to minister for the blessing of the rest, "as good stewards of the grace of God." A steward is held accountable to fulfill faithfully the trust committed to him by his master.

They who speak, addressing the church when assembled together, are not to give out their own or other men's theories, but are to speak as the oracles of God, declaring only that which He has revealed. Those who minister (or serve) in any capacity are to do it according to the ability God gives, so that in all things He may be glorified through Christ Jesus to whom all praise and dominion eternally belong.

Suffering as a Christian

The name *Christian* is not found very often in the New Testament, but is the distinctive title of those who belong to Christ. We read of it in Acts 11:26 where it was conferred upon the Gentile believers at Antioch by divine authority; for the word *called* there literally means "oracularly called," and therefore it was not the Antiochians alone who bestowed this name upon the believers, but God Himself who so designated them. That it has become their well-known appellation is evident from Acts 26:28, where we read that King Agrippa exclaimed, "Almost thou persuadest me to be a Christian!" When Peter wrote this letter some years later he uses it as the commonly recognized name of the pilgrim company, and he tells us that it is praiseworthy to suffer as a Christian.

> Beloved, think it not strange concerning the fiery trial which is to try you, as though some strange thing happened unto you: but rejoice, inasmuch as ye are partakers of Christ's sufferings; that, when his glory shall be revealed, ye may be glad also with exceeding joy. If ye be reproached for the name of Christ, happy are ye; for the spirit of glory and of God resteth upon you: on their part he is evil spoken of, but on your part he is glorified. But let none of you suffer as a murderer, or as a thief, or as an evildoer, or as a busybody in other men's matters. Yet if any man suffer as a Christian, let him not be ashamed; but let him glorify God on this behalf. For the time is come that judgment must begin at the house of God: and if it first begin at us, what shall the end be of them that obey not the gospel of God? And if the righteous scarcely be saved, where shall the ungodly and the sinner appear? Wherefore let them that suffer according to the will of God commit the keeping of their souls to him in well doing, as unto a faithful Creator. (vv. 12–19)

In verse 12 Peter writes of "the fiery trial which is to try you." Primarily, the reference was to the great suffering that the Jews—whether Christian or not—were about to undergo in connection with the fulfillment of our Lord's prophecy concerning Jerusalem's destruction, shortly to take place (Luke 21:20–24). But it also has reference to the horrors of the Roman persecutions, which were to continue for two terrible centuries. The words are applicable to every time of trial and persecution.

"Partakers of Christ's sufferings" (v. 13). The believer suffers in fellowship with his Lord. Our Lord has told us to expect this (John 15:18–21). We cannot be partakers of His atoning sufferings. They stand alone: none but He could endure the penalty for our sins and so make propitiation, in order that we might be forgiven. But we share His sufferings for righteousness' sake.

"Reproached for the name of Christ" (v. 14). No one can be true to Christ and loved by the world-system, for everything that Jesus taught condemns the present order and leads ungodly men to hate Him and His people. But he who suffers for Christ's sake now is assured of glory hereafter, which will fully answer to the shame now endured. "On their part He is evil spoken of, but on your part He is glorified." The reproach of the world should not deter the Christian. He need not expect the approval of those who reject and misunderstand his Savior. It is his responsibility so to live as to give the lie to the false reports of the ungodly and so to glorify the One whose name they spurn.

No believer should ever suffer as "a busybody in other men's matters" (v. 15). Notice the company in which the busybody is placed. He is linked with murderers, thieves, and evildoers of every description, and that for a very good reason; for the busybody steals men's reputations, seeks to assassinate their good names, and by his calumniations works all manner of evil. The follower of Christ is called upon to be careful never to misbehave so as to deserve the ill will of the wicked. He is not to be dishonest or corrupt in life, nor to be given to gossipy interference in other people's affairs. Thus by a holy and righteous life, he will adorn the gospel of Christ (Phil. 1:27–28).

"If any man suffer as a Christian, let him not be ashamed" (v. 16). None needs to be ashamed to suffer because of his faithfulness to the hallowed name he bears. The disciples, as we have noticed already, were called Christians first at Antioch (Acts 11:26), and this name has clung to them ever since. It signifies their union with Christ, and therefore is a name in which to glory, however the world may despise it! Let us therefore never be ashamed of this name and all that it implies, but be prepared to suffer because of it, knowing that we may thus glorify the God who has drawn us to Himself and saves us through His blessed Son, who bore our sins in His own body on the tree (1 Peter 2:24).

"Judgment must begin at the house of God" (v. 17). Our Father God does not pass over the failures of His people, but disciplines them in order that they may be careful to walk in obedience to His Word. If He is thus particular in chastening His own, how solemn will be the judgment of "them that obey not the gospel," but persist to the end in rejecting the Savior He has provided!

"If the righteous scarcely be saved" (v. 18), that is, if the righteous have to endure chastening at the hand of God and persecution at the hand of the world, what will it mean for unsaved and impenitent men to answer before the judgment throne for their persistence in refusing His grace?

"Commit the keeping of their souls . . . in well doing, as unto a faithful Creator" (v. 19). However hard the way and however perplexing their experiences, the suffering Christian may look up to God in confidence, knowing he can rely upon the divine love and faithfulness, and assured that all will work out for blessing at last.

Throughout the entire Christian era, which is that of the dispensation of the grace of God (Eph. 3:2), believers in Christ are called out from the world and are responsible to live for the glory of Him who has saved them. But though separated from the surrounding evil, they are not to shut themselves up as in a monastery or convent in order to be protected from defilement, but are to go forth as God's messengers into that very world from which they have been delivered, preaching to all men everywhere the gospel, which is God's offer of salvation through the finished work of His beloved Son. Whatever suffering or affliction this entails is to be borne cheerfully for His sake, knowing that He will reward abundantly for all endured, when He returns in glory. His church is to be in the world, but not of it, witnessing rather against its evil, and offering pardon through the cross.

Tertullian declared that the blood of the martyrs is the seed of the church. This has been demonstrated over and over again. Persecution can never destroy the church of God. The more it is called to suffer for Christ, the stronger it becomes. It is internal strife and carelessness in life that endangers it. But so virile is the life it possesses that even this has never been permitted to destroy it, for although its outward testimony has at times been ruined by such things, God has always kept alive a witnessing remnant to stand for the truth of His Word.

CHAPTER 5

THE END OF THE WAY

1 Peter 5

The path of suffering, both for Christ and for His followers, ends in glory. Peter has a special word for his fellow elders, to whom was committed the care of the flock of God, and who were, as we know, specially exposed to the assaults of the enemy.

> The elders which are among you I exhort, who am also an elder, and a witness of the sufferings of Christ, and also a partaker of the glory that shall be revealed: feed the flock of God which is among you, taking the oversight thereof, not by constraint, but willingly; not for filthy lucre, but of a ready mind; neither as being lords over God's heritage, but being examples to the flock. And when the chief Shepherd shall appear, ye shall receive a crown of glory that fadeth not away. (vv. 1–4)

Note the expression, "the elders which are among you." There is no suggestion here of a clerical order ruling arbitrarily over the laity. These elders were mature, godly men, upon whom rested the responsibility of watching over the souls of believers, as those for whom they must give an account (Heb. 13:17). Peter links himself with them, "who am also an elder," or "who am a *co-presbyter.*" If Peter was ever a Pope he never knew it! He took his place as one with his elder brethren in sharing the ministry for the edification of the saints, even though he was one of the original twelve, and so a witness of the sufferings of Christ; and he was yet to be partaker of the glory that shall be revealed at the Lord's second advent.

He admonishes the elders to feed, not fleece, "the flock of God which is among you." They were to feed the people by ministering the truth of God as made known in His holy Word. What a grievous thing it is when men, professing to be servants of Christ, set before the sheep and lambs of His flock unscriptural teachings that cannot edify but only mislead!

Not as pressed unwillingly into a service that was a hard, unwelcome task, were these elders to take the oversight; nor yet for what money was to be gained thereby, but as serving the Lord with all readiness of mind. Neither were they to become ecclesiastical lords, dominating over God's heritage. Think of the hierarchy that has been developed in the professing body, with its priests, lord-bishops, cardinals known as "princes of the church," and all the other dignitaries who rule as with an iron hand those under their jurisdiction! Could anything be more opposed to what Peter teaches here? Yet some call him the first Pope!

Whatever authority the elders have springs from lives of godliness and subjection to the Lord. They are to be examples to the flock, those whom the sheep of Christ may safely follow.

Their reward will be sure when they reach the end of the way. Then they shall give account of their service to the Chief Shepherd at His glorious appearing, and His own blessed hands will bestow upon each faithful under-shepherd an unfading victor's wreath of glory—the token of His pleasure in the service they have done as unto Him.

Grace Operative on the Journey

We have seen that throughout this epistle Peter dwells on the grace of God as that which enables the believer to triumph in all circumstances. He stresses this most definitely in the concluding section of this epistle.

Likewise, ye younger, submit yourselves unto the elder. Yea, all of you be subject one to another, and be clothed with humility: for God resisteth the proud, and giveth grace to the humble. Humble yourselves therefore under the mighty hand of God, that he may exalt you in due time: casting all your care upon him; for he careth for you. Be sober, be vigilant; because your adversary the devil, as a roaring lion, walketh about, seeking whom he may devour: whom resist steadfast in the faith, knowing that the same afflictions are accomplished in your brethren that are in the world. But the God of all grace, who hath called us unto his eternal glory by Christ Jesus, after that ye have suffered a while, make you perfect, stablish, strengthen, settle you. To him be glory and dominion for ever and ever. Amen. By Silvanus, a faithful brother unto you, as I suppose, I have written briefly, exhorting, and testifying that this is the true grace of God wherein ye stand. The church that is at Babylon, elected together with you, saluteth you; and so doth Marcus my son. Greet ye one another with a kiss of charity. Peace be with you all that are in Christ Jesus. Amen. (vv. 5–14)

It is as we walk in subjection to Him who is meek and lowly in heart that we can appreciate the preciousness of that grace that He gives to the humble. Pride is a barrier to all spiritual progress. In the Christian company it should have no place. None should ever be puffed up against others. All are to be submissive to one another, not only the younger to the elder, as is befitting, but each to his brethren, and all clothed with humility; for God sets Himself against the proud and haughty, but ministers all needed grace to enable the meek to overcome, no matter what difficulties they are called upon to face.

"Humble yourselves therefore . . . that He may exalt you in due time" (v. 6). We are to take the lowly place of unquestioning submission to the will of God now, knowing on the authority of His Word that in the day of manifestation He will take note of all we have endured for His name's sake, and He will then give abundant reward.

"He careth for you" (v. 7). It is of all-importance to realize that God's heart is ever toward His own. He is no indifferent spectator of our suffering. He feels for us in all our afflictions and bids us cast every care upon Him, assured that He is concerned about all we have to endure. Weymouth has rendered the last part of this verse, "It matters to God about you." How precious to realize this!

"Your adversary the devil . . . walketh about" (v. 8). Satan is a real being, a malignant personality, the bitter enemy of God and man. But when we refuse to give place to the Devil, standing firmly at the cross, he flees from us, and his power is broken.

"Whom resist" (v. 9). We are to stand against all the Devil's suggestions, "steadfast in the faith," battling for the truth committed to us. Neither are we alone in this: our brethren everywhere have the same enemy to face.

"After that ye have suffered a while" (v. 10). We grow by suffering. Only thus can God's plan of conformity to Christ be carried out. But all is ordered of Him. He will not permit one trial too many. When His purpose is fulfilled we shall be perfected and established in His grace.

"To him be glory and dominion for ever and ever" (v. 11). The victory will be His at last. All evil will be put down; Satan will be shut up in his eternal prison house. Suffering then will be only a memory, and God will be glorified in all His saints, and His dominion established over all the universe.

In verse 12 Peter mentions the name of his amanuensis, Silvanus, whom Peter regarded as a faithful brother to them and to himself. He may be the same Silas, or Silvanus, who accompanied Paul on his second missionary journey; or he may have been another of the same, not uncommon, name. The theme of the entire epistle is here declared to be "the true grace of God wherein ye stand." As intimated in our introduction, while these words are much like those of Paul in Romans 5:2, "This grace wherein we stand," the meaning is different. Paul writes of our standing in grace before God; Peter testifies to the power of grace that enables us to stand in the hour of trial, neither giving place to the Devil nor disheartened by suffering and persecution. There are abundant stores of grace from which we may draw freely for strength to meet every emergency as we pursue our pilgrim way.

This letter was written at Babylon, which Romanists claim was pagan Rome, but it seems more likely it was, as the Nestorian Church has held from the beginning, Babylon on the Euphrates, where many Jews dwelt to whom Peter ministered—or as the Coptic Church holds, with apparently less evidence, a new Babylon in Egypt, near to the present city of Cairo. Wherever it was, the church there joined Peter in salutations to the scattered Christians throughout Asia Minor. Mark, too, participated in this. He is identical with the John Mark who was the companion for a time of Paul and Barnabas, and who, though unfaithful at first, became accredited later to Paul's own satisfaction (2 Tim. 4:11). According to some very early writers Mark accompanied Peter in later years and wrote his gospel in collaboration with the venerable apostle, under the Holy Spirit's guidance.

The epistle closes with a benediction quite different from those that bring Paul's letters to an end. Paul always wrote of grace: Peter bids the saints greet one another with a kiss of love, and prays that peace may be with all that are in

Christ Jesus. These three final words are significant. We ordinarily think of them as characteristic of Paul's writings. He uses the expressions "in Christ" and "in Christ Jesus" with great frequency. Peter joins with Paul in speaking of the saints in this blessed relationship. They are no longer in the flesh or in Adam; they are new by new birth and the gift of the indwelling Spirit in Christ Jesus, and so a new creation.

PART 3

2 PETER

INTRODUCTION

How much time elapsed between the writing of the two Petrine epistles we have no way of determining. But certainly when one says, "This second epistle . . . I now write unto you" (3:1), it implies that the first one had been sent just a short time before. This was true in regard to Paul's two letters to the Corinthians, those to the Thessalonians, and the two pastoral letters to Timothy.

Paul was, in all probability, already with the Lord when Peter wrote, or else he was enduring his last imprisonment just prior to his martyrdom; for Peter mentions "all his epistles" as being in circulation already. This is important, inasmuch as some have sought to minimize the importance of Peter's written ministry in order to enhance the value of Paul's letters. But God does not set one apostle against another in this way. All Scripture is divinely inspired, and all is profitable. And as Peter was led of God to write these letters possibly after Paul's ministry had come to a close, we dare not under-estimate their value. They contain precious and important truth that the church can neglect only at its peril.

It is true that in early days some sought to cast doubt on the authenticity of this second epistle, but there can be no question now as to this. It bears every mark of inspiration and, as such, has been accepted by the church since the second century at least, and by many reliable witnesses from the first, beginning, that is, from the time when it was first circulated, somewhere about A.D. 66 to 70.

Like all second epistles it is corrective. In the first epistles we hear the voice of the teacher. As a rule in second epistles it is rather the prophet or the exhorter who speaks.

The theme of this letter is "Faithfulness in a Day of Apostasy." The three chapters form three distinct divisions.

I. Chapter 1: The Blessings Bestowed upon Believers Through the Righteousness of God
   A. Blessings received and growth in grace (vv. 1–11)
   B. The hope of the coming kingdom (vv. 12–21)
II. Chapter 2: Increasing Apostasy and the Call to Righteousness
   A. Lessons from the past for the present age (vv. 1–10)
   B. Characteristics of apostate teachers (vv. 11–17)
   C. Turning away from the truth to the false philosophies of the world (vv. 18–22)
III. Chapter 3: Looking on to the Culmination
   A. Forgetting the past and denying the future (vv. 1–7)
   B. The day of the Lord and the day of God (vv. 8–14)
   C. A final warning (vv. 15–18)

We should be very grateful to God that He has given such a faithful portrayal of conditions that He foresaw from the first, in order that we might not be disheartened when these things actually developed in the professing church.

CHAPTER 1

The Blessings Bestowed upon Believers Through the Righteousness of God

2 Peter 1

As we begin our consideration of this second epistle it is well for us to remember that it is in the nature of a final message from Christ's venerable servant, the apostle Peter, who wrote in view of his forthcoming martyrdom, in order to warn believers of the oncoming flood of error and apostasy that was to sweep over Christendom, and that would necessitate real confidence in God and His Word on the part of those who were to be called upon to meet such disturbing conditions.

In a very blessed way the Spirit of God first puts before us the blessings that are ours as Christians, and the importance of growing in grace and in the knowledge of Christ that we may have strength to stand against the evils threatening the church.

Blessings Received and Growth in Grace

Simon Peter, a servant and an apostle of Jesus Christ, to them that have obtained like precious faith with us through the righteousness of God and our Savior Jesus Christ: grace and peace be multiplied unto you through the knowledge of God, and of Jesus our Lord, according as his divine power hath given unto us all things that pertain unto life and godliness, through the knowledge of him that hath called us to glory and virtue: whereby are given unto us exceeding great and precious promises: that by these ye might be partakers of the divine nature, having escaped the corruption that is in the world through lust. And beside this, giving all diligence, add to your faith virtue; and to virtue knowledge; and to knowledge temperance; and to temperance patience; and to patience godliness; and to godliness brotherly kindness; and to brotherly kindness charity. For if these things be in you, and abound, they make you that ye shall neither be barren nor unfruitful in the knowledge of our Lord Jesus Christ. But he that lacketh these things is blind, and cannot see afar off, and hath forgotten that he was purged from his old sins. Wherefore the rather, brethren, give diligence to make your calling and election sure: for if ye do these things, ye shall never fall: for so an entrance shall be ministered unto you abundantly into the everlasting kingdom of our Lord and Savior Jesus Christ. (vv. 1–11)

Peter addresses himself to the same scattered saints as mentioned in his first letter, but without indicating them according to the lands of their dispersion, as before. But verse 1 of chapter 3 makes it clear that this second letter was sent to the same persons as the first one.

He simply writes to them as those "that have obtained like precious faith with us through the righteousness of God and our Savior Jesus Christ."

In verse 1 note the word *precious*, which we have seen is one of frequent occurrence in his letters. He writes of faith through the righteousness of God and our Savior Jesus Christ. This stands out in remarkable contrast to the theme so frequently dwelt upon by the apostle Paul—"The righteousness which is of God by faith" (Phil. 3:9). This expression refers to that righteousness that God imputes to all who believe on the Lord Jesus Christ, who has met every claim of the throne of God in regard to the sin question. But Peter dwells on an altogether different aspect of things: since Christ has died for all men, God, in His righteousness, has opened the door of faith to everyone who desires to enter. It would be unrighteous of God to refuse to save anyone who desired to avail himself of the result of the work of the cross. The very righteousness of God demands that faith be extended to all men. This is the very opposite of what some High Calvinists teach. They would have us believe that faith itself is a gift that God grants only to a limited number, that all men have not faith because it is not the will of God that they should have it. This is the very opposite of the teaching of the Holy Scriptures. God desires that all men should be saved and come to the knowledge of the truth. The reason that some men have not faith is that they will not give heed to the Word, and "faith cometh by hearing, and hearing by the Word of God" (Rom. 10:17). Where men are ready to hear, God can be depended upon to see that they obtain this precious gift of faith. It would be unrighteous in Him to do otherwise.

In the second verse we have again the apostolic salutation in which Peter prays that grace and peace might be multiplied unto the believers through the full knowledge, or super-knowledge, of God and of Jesus Christ our Lord. This is a completeness of knowledge that only the Holy Spirit Himself can give. It is interesting to observe how frequently Peter uses mathematical terms in both his epistles. The word *multiplied*, for example, is found not only here but also in 1:2 of the first epistle, where it is used in a similar connection. There is an abundance of grace and peace available for all who rest in simplicity of heart upon the testimony God has given. His divine power has bequeathed to us everything that is necessary for spiritual life and piety, but this can never be divorced from the knowledge of Him who has called us, not exactly *to* glory and virtue, but by His glories and virtues. In other words, it is as we become better acquainted with God revealed in Christ that we grow in grace and become more like Him with whom our souls are occupied.

In verse 1 the apostle is speaking of precious faith; in verse 4 he reminds us that God has given us His surpassing great and precious promises. As we lay hold of these and dare to act in accordance with them, we who have been born again by believing the gospel, manifest the divine nature in our practical lives, having thus found deliverance from the corruption into which the whole world has been brought through lust, that is, through unlawful desire; for the word "lust" should never be limited simply to fleshly concupiscence, but includes covetousness and every sort of yearning after that which God, in His infinite love and wisdom, has forbidden. As we thus act upon the truth of the Word, we will be prepared for that which follows in verses 5 to 7. Here again, according to our Authorized Version, Peter writes from a mathematical standpoint as he tells us of the graces that should be added to our faith. A better figure perhaps is that of a growing tree: an acorn, for instance, falls into the ground; the seed germinates, strikes its roots downward, and its branches shoot upward; and that acorn becomes an entire oak tree with all its various parts. Faith is like the acorn—a living faith, that should characterize us as devoted Christians. So Peter says, "Have in your faith virtue." The virtue of which he speaks here is not simply chastity, as some might think, but it is really valor, which is the outstanding virtue of a soldier, and we are called to be soldiers of Christ. Then he adds, "And in virtue knowledge." There can be no proper growth without a deepened understanding of spiritual realities. "In knowledge temperance," or self-control. A Christian who gives way to evil tempers, or careless habits of any kind, is not growing in grace in self-control. "In temperance patience"—that which enables one to endure without complaining, even though exposed to circumstances that are very distasteful to the natural man. "In patience godliness," which is really "God-likeness," or true piety, as we have seen in considering the first epistle. In godliness we will have brotherly kindness—consideration for all who belong, through the grace of God, to the Christian brotherhood. Last of all he adds, "In brotherly kindness charity," or "love." This is the full fruitage of faith, for Paul tells us that faith worketh by love (Gal. 5:6).

If these things are found in a believer, and that not in scanty measure but in abundance, the effect is to make him neither idle nor unfruitful in the knowledge of our Lord Jesus Christ. Our Authorized Version renders it, "Neither barren nor unfruitful," but these terms are synonymous as ordinarily used. "Idle" or "inactivity" is a better rendering of the original than the word *barren*. One who does not manifest these fruits of faith is designated here as blind, or myopic. He is unable to discern spiritual things; and though once truly born of God, he forgets the sins from which he has been purged and is likely to lapse into them again, thus coming under the government of God because of failure to go on with the Lord.

Peter concludes this exhortation in verses 10 and 11 by urging those to whom he writes to give diligence to make their calling and election sure, that is, in the sense of manifestation. No one has any reason to believe that one is numbered among the elect of God unless he is characterized by faith that brings forth fruit unto God; but where this is true there will be constant victory over tendencies toward evil, "For if ye do these things, ye shall never fall." A promise is given that the final result will be an abundant entrance into the everlasting kingdom of our Lord and Savior Jesus Christ. Observe, it is not an entrance into heaven as such that is here put before us. Heaven is the Father's house, and to that all believers have exactly the same title; it is the home of the Father's children, and the weakest and feeblest of saints will be as welcome there as the strongest and most useful. But the everlasting kingdom is another sphere: it speaks of reward, and our place in the kingdom is determined by our devotion to Christ in this scene.

The Hope of the Coming Kingdom

In verses 12 to 14 Peter refers to what the Lord had told him concerning his martyrdom.

> Wherefore I will not be negligent to put you always in remembrance of these things, though ye know them, and be established in the present truth. Yea, I think it meet, as long as I am in this tabernacle, to stir you up by putting you in remembrance; knowing that shortly I must put off this my tabernacle, even as our Lord Jesus Christ hath showed me. (vv. 12–14)

Jesus had made it very plain, in speaking to Peter on that morning by the seaside when He publicly restored him to the place of apostleship, that in his old age he should die for Christ's name's sake. Many years had passed since that memorable conversation, and Peter was now well advanced in years. He knew he could not remain much longer in this world; therefore, he was desirous of leaving behind what written ministry he could in order that the saints might be helped by it and established in the needed truth for the present hour of testing.

Notice how he puts it in verse 12: "Wherefore I will not be negligent to put you always in remembrance of these things, though ye know them, and be established in the present truth." He was not writing to young believers who were ignorant of the precious things of which he desired to remind them. But he knew the value of repetition because we forget so easily. He considered it suitable or important, therefore, as long as he remained in his fleshly tabernacle—that is, in his body—to stir up the saints by bringing these things to their remembrance. And he knew well that in a very short time he would be obliged to put off his tabernacle in accordance with what the Lord Jesus had revealed to him. Observe that he had no thought of going to sleep in his tabernacle as some modern materialists, masquerading under the Christian name, would have us believe. While alive on the earth Peter himself, the real man, dwelt in the body that he calls his tabernacle; when death came he would move out of the tabernacle, and, as Paul puts it, go home "to be with Christ; which is far better" (Phil. 1:23). A comparison of this passage with 2 Corinthians 5:1–10 will prove most illuminating in connection with the truth concerning the believer in life and in death. Scripture leaves no room whatever for the doctrine of the sleep of the soul, but only the sleep of the body until the Lord Jesus returns, when the dead will be raised and the living changed (1 Thess. 4:15–17).

We have seen already that these two epistles of Peter were linked with two great experiences in his life during the earthly ministry of our blessed Lord. We have considered the first one in connection with the Lord's declaration as to the building of His church upon the truth that He is the Son of the living God. Now Peter refers to that other great experience that took place on the Mount of Transfiguration.

> Moreover I will endeavor that ye may be able after my decease to have these things always in remembrance. For we have not followed cunningly devised fables, when we made known unto you the power and coming of our Lord Jesus Christ, but were eyewitnesses of his majesty. For he received from God the Father honor and glory, when there came such a voice to him from the excellent glory, This is my beloved Son, in whom I am well pleased. And this voice which came from heaven we heard, when we were with him in the holy mount. (vv. 15–18)

Guided by the Holy Spirit, Peter was unfolding truth that the Lord could use in after days for the comfort and sanctification of believers. He speaks of his own death as an exodus. The word rendered "decease" is really the same as the title of the second book of the Old Testament. This agrees with what we have pointed out already. At death Peter would be moving out from the body and going into the presence of the Lord. In view of the imminence of this event he endeavored to make certain things clear that would be for the enlightenment of the saints. He denies having followed cunningly devised fables when he and other inspired apostles had made known the power and the coming of the Lord Jesus Christ. They were eyewitnesses of His majesty when, on the Mount of Transfiguration, He was metamorphosed before them, and the glory from within shone out through the very raiment that He wore. Moses and Elijah appeared with Him at that time, as we know, and spoke of His decease, which He was to accomplish at Jerusalem. When Peter suggested making three booths or tabernacles that they might tarry there, a cloud covered the scene, and a voice came from the Excellent Glory, saying, "This is my beloved Son, in whom I am well pleased" (Matt. 3:17). This was not a dream, neither was it the effects of a wrought-up imagination; but Peter said, "This voice which came from heaven we heard, when we were with him in the holy mount." It was there that God vouchsafed to Peter, James, and John a view of the kingdom in miniature. They beheld the Lord as He will yet be when He returns to take His great power and reign.

What they saw and heard on the Mount confirmed the word of prophecy given in the Old Testament. To that, Peter refers in the closing verses.

> We have also a more sure word of prophecy; whereunto ye do well that ye take heed, as unto a light that shineth in a dark place, until the day dawn, and the day star arise in your hearts: knowing this first, that no prophecy of the scripture is of any private interpretation. For the prophecy came not in old time by the will of man: but holy men of God spake as they were moved by the Holy Ghost. (vv. 19–21)

As we have it in the opening clause of the nineteenth verse in the Authorized Version, we might suppose that Peter was telling us that the word of prophecy was even more sure than the Father's voice or the glory that the disciples beheld; but that is not exactly what he says. We might better read, "We have also the word of prophecy confirmed, and to this prophetic word believers do well to take heed in their hearts, for the lamp of prophecy is as a light that shineth in a dark place." It is intended by God to illumine our paths and give light in our souls until the day dawn and the day star arise at the coming of our Lord Jesus Christ. It is all important, then, that we give heed to that which has been revealed in the prophetic Scriptures; but on the other hand, we need to be careful lest we take some of these Scriptures out of their connection and endeavor to interpret them according to specific incidents, rather than in accordance with the entire plan of God, as revealed in His Word. No prophecy of the Scripture is of its own interpretation; none can be fully understood apart from the rest. Rome takes this condemnation of any private interpretation as forbidding the individual believer to study the Word of God for himself and be guided by it directly, rather than through the interpretation put upon it by the church and its councils. But it is not that at all that Peter had in mind, but rather the folly of taking some portion of the prophetic Word and endeavoring to apply it to some special circumstances, while failing to note its context and its connection with the general trend of prophecy as a whole. This is a snare to which many students of prophecy have been exposed, and numbers of them have failed at this very point. It means much to see that prophecy is one whole, and "known unto God are all his works from the beginning of the world" (Acts 15:18); and "the prophecy came not in old time by the will of man: but holy men of God spake as they were moved [or borne along] by the Holy Ghost." While it has not pleased Him to give in any Old Testament book a complete unfolding of the future concerning the glorious kingdom of Messiah and the events leading up to it, yet by searching the writings of all the prophets and comparing Scripture with Scripture one is able to see, with at least a measure of clearness, the wonderful harmony of the prophetic Word and the marvelous way in which God is unfolding that purpose of the ages, which will result eventually in heading up all things in Christ, when, in the dispensation of the fullness of times, He will be manifest as King of kings and Lord of lords.

CHAPTER 2

INCREASING APOSTASY AND THE CALL TO RIGHTEOUSNESS

2 Peter 2

False doctrines had begun already to make serious inroads into the churches scattered throughout the world, as Paul's later letters give evidence, and as that of Jude also bears witness. Peter had this in mind when he gave his final message to the saints; but he foresaw even greater apostasy in days to come, and so gave an inspired word of warning in order that the believers might not be carried away by the personality and persuasiveness of false teachers masquerading as servants of Christ.

The close connection between this chapter and the epistle of Jude has been noted often, and has given rise in some quarters to the idea that one is but a mutilated copy of the other. What we need to keep in mind is that the Holy Spirit Himself inspired both of these writers to portray conditions that the church of God would have to face in years to come. While they cover the same ground to some extent, there is one very striking difference between them: Peter emphasizes the spread of unscriptural theories whereas Jude dwells more particularly upon the effects of these, turning the grace of God into lasciviousness. Thus they give a twofold warning designed to save the elect of God from being misled. When once we realize that the Holy Spirit Himself is the author of all Scripture, we will not be surprised to find that He speaks in similar terms through different servants; in fact, we should naturally expect this. "The testimony of two men is true," we are told; and by this double testimony God emphasizes those things that we need to keep in mind.

Lessons from the Past for the Present Age

In verses 1 to 10 Peter turns our minds back to conditions that prevailed in former days and that have important lessons for us. Let us look at this passage with particular care.

> But there were false prophets also among the people, even as there shall be false teachers among you, who privily shall bring in damnable heresies, even denying the Lord that bought them and bring upon themselves swift destruction. And many shall follow their pernicious ways; by reason of whom the way of truth shall be evil spoken of. And through covetousness shall they with feigned words make merchandise of you: whose judgment now of a long time lingereth not, and their damnation slumbereth not. For if God spared not the angels that sinned, but cast them down to hell, and delivered them into chains of darkness, to be reserved unto judgment; and spared not the old world, but saved Noah the eighth person, a preacher of righteousness, bringing in the flood upon the world of the ungodly; and turning the cities of Sodom and Gomorrah into ashes condemned them with an overthrow, making them an ensample unto those that after should live ungodly; and delivered just Lot, vexed with the filthy conversation of the wicked: (for that righteous man dwelling among them, in seeing and hearing, vexed his righteous soul from day to day with their unlawful deeds;) the Lord knoweth how to deliver the godly out of temptations, and to reserve the unjust unto the day of judgment to be punished: but chiefly them that walk after the flesh in the lust of uncleanness, and despise government. Presumptuous are they, self-willed, they are not afraid to speak evil of dignities. (vv. 1–10)

After God brought Israel out of Egypt, false prophets rose up from time to time—from the days when Korah, Dathan, and Abiram opposed Moses right on down to the period immediately preceding the captivity of Israel and Judah under Assyria and Babylon respectively—to controvert the truth, which He revealed through His specially anointed servants. God's true servants were opposed by these false prophets who sought to foist their own dreams upon the people, instead of the truth as declared by those who were divinely enlightened. Similar conditions had begun already to prevail in Christian circles even in apostolic times, and God foresaw that false teachers would rise up throughout all the centuries prior to the coming again of our Lord Jesus Christ. These false teachers come in under cover. They bring in heresies privately or secretly. It is never customary for teachers of error to declare and oppose the truth openly in the beginning. As a rule they work in an underhanded way, seeking to gain the confidence of God's people before they make known their real views. Such false teachers often hide their doctrinal peculiarities by using orthodox terms to which, however, they attach an altogether different meaning than that which is ordinarily accepted. Once having wormed their way into the confidence of the people of God they go to the limit, even denying the Lord who bought them, and so exposing themselves to the judgment of God. If they alone were thus dealt with it would be comparatively a small thing, but the sad result of their unscriptural ministry is that the weak and uninstructed readily follow the pernicious ways of these misleading representatives of Satan, and because of this, the way of truth—that is, "the faith which was once delivered unto the saints"—is derided and evil spoken of.

We could instance many such cases today in various circles where the greatest and most precious things of God are spurned and held up to ridicule by those who have imbibed false views through giving heed to these heretical teachers. Heresy is like leaven. As the apostle Paul tells us when combating Jewish legality, which was spreading among the Galatians, "A little leaven leaveneth the whole lump" (Gal. 5:9). Leaven is corruption, and its nature is to corrupt all with which it comes in contact. So it is with false doctrine.

Back of every system of error is the sin of covetousness. Men seek to draw away disciples after themselves in order that they may make gain of them, and so as Peter here explains, "Through covetousness shall they with feigned words make merchandise of you." If it were not for the money question one wonders how long many systems of error would survive. Alas, that any should be so sordid as to seek to enrich themselves through the credulity of the souls whom they lead astray. The judgment of such is like a Damocles sword hanging over their heads, and though it seems to slumber for the moment it will not be long before it falls with terrible effect upon all such blind leaders of the blind.

In verse 4 we are referred to the apostasy of angels. These who were created innocent, followed the lead of Satan and sinned even in heaven. God has spared them not, though they were beings of so high an order; but He cast them down to Tartarus, which is the lowest depth of hell. There they are held in chains of darkness, awaiting the final judgment. It seems very clear that Scripture contemplates two distinct angelic apostasies. While Satan is the leader in both, yet they did not each occur at the same time. Satan himself is not yet bound in Tartarus, nor will he be until he is cast into the bottomless pit, which is prior to the millennial reign of our Lord Jesus Christ, as we learn from Revelation 20:1. The angels that followed him in his first rebellion seem to be identical with the demons who have ever been the opponents of the truth of God and who were specially active in opposition to the Lord Jesus Christ when He was here on earth. Satan is called the Prince of the Power of the Air, and he and his cohorts are still at large and are described as wicked spirits in the heavenlies. They are thus able to carry on constant warfare against the saints. The sin of the angels mentioned here in 2 Peter, and also in the epistle of Jude, seems to be of a special character and may be that which is referred to in Genesis 6:2, where we read, "The sons of God saw the daughters of men that they were fair; and they took them wives of all which they chose." This is admittedly a very mysterious passage, but many have understood it to mean that certain angelic beings, such as are referred to in the book of Job as "sons of God," forsook their own habitation and came down to earth and took possession of the bodies of men, stirring them up to unlawful lusts, which resulted in that corruption and violence that brought about the deluge.

When that flood spread over all the world of the ungodly, destroying those who persisted in their opposition to the truth, God saved Noah and his family, making eight persons in all. Noah is spoken of here as a preacher of righteousness. He preached, doubtless, not only by word of mouth but also by his actions. It has been well said that every spike that Noah drove into the ark was a sermon to that ungodly generation, declaring that judgment was about to fall.

Next we have reference to the judgment of Sodom and Gomorrah. These cities gave themselves over to such vileness that God could no longer tolerate their inhabitants, and so He overthrew them, destroying them with fire from heaven, making them an example or a warning unto those who should in after days live in the same ungodly manner. When God overthrew these cities of the plains, He delivered just Lot, who for years had dwelt in Sodom, though distressed by the filthy behavior of the wicked. We might never have thought of Lot as deserving to be called a righteous man, but the Holy Spirit so speaks of him here. He was a righteous man living in a wrong place; as a result he was in a constant state of vexation; his righteous soul was disturbed continually by what he heard and saw among the people with whom he dwelt. It is noticeable that though he is here designated as "just" and "righteous," we do not find his name in the eleventh chapter of the epistle to the Hebrews. It never could have been said that "by faith Lot dwelt in Sodom": it was rather lack of faith that took him there. He hoped thereby to better his worldly circumstances. Finally, when the judgment fell he was saved out of it all but so as by fire. The conflagration destroyed everything for which he had labored during all those years that he had lived in Sodom.

Even as the Lord delivered Noah and Lot before the judgments fell, so now He never forgets His own; and He knows how to deliver the godly out of trials and temptations, persecutions, and tribulations of every kind, and to reserve the unjust until the day of judgment to be punished. Often it seems as though the more wicked men are, the more they prosper in this world; whereas the righteous suffer almost continuously. But God permits trial to come to His own for their discipline; whereas He allows the ungodly to have their fling now, as we say, but they will be judged according to their deeds when at last they appear before Him.

In verse 10 we have certain characteristics brought before us that mark out these false teachers. In the untruths that they proclaim there is no power to hold the flesh in check, so they secretly and often openly live in the lust of uncleanness, making excuses for their evil behavior. They despise authority and do not desire to be subject to anyone. They are presumptuous, venturing to attempt to explore mysteries that even the most godly dare not look into; they are self-willed, determined to have their own way, and are not afraid to speak evil of those of highest rank, so lifted up are they in their own pride and conceit.

Characteristics of Apostate Teachers

In verses 11 to 17 we have further evidence of the true nature of these apostates.

> Whereas angels, which are greater in power and might, bring not railing
> accusation against them before the Lord. But these, as natural brute
> beasts, made to be taken and destroyed, speak evil of the things that

they understand not; and shall utterly perish in their own corruption; and shall receive the reward of unrighteousness, as they that count it pleasure to riot in the day time. Spots they are and blemishes, sporting themselves with their own deceivings while they feast with you; haying eyes full of adultery, and that cannot cease from sin; beguiling unstable souls: an heart they have exercised with covetous practices; cursed children: which have forsaken the right way, and are gone astray, following the way of Balaam the son of Bosor, who loved the wages of unrighteousness; but was rebuked for his iniquity: the dumb ass speaking with man's voice forbad the madness of the prophet. These are wells without water, clouds that are carried with a tempest; to whom the mist of darkness is reserved for ever. (vv. 11–17)

While these ungodly men vaunt themselves against all authority, human, angelic, or divine, the elect angels—those who have been preserved by God from falling into sin, who are greater far in power and might than men here on the earth—do not presume to bring railing accusations even against those of their own order who have apostatized from God. Jude tells us that Michael the archangel did not bring against Satan a railing accusation but simply said, "The Lord rebuke thee." But these apostate leaders behave like natural brute beasts who are made to be taken and destroyed. These brutes, not possessing intelligence, act in accordance with their own vicious appetites and are imitated by the false teachers against whom Peter warns, who rail against things that God has made known in His Word but that they do not understand. In refusing the truth they, of necessity, will be left to perish in their own corruption, and in due time will be rewarded according to the unrighteousness of their lives. They have lived as though their greatest object was to satisfy the desires of their own hearts. They have counted it a pleasure to riot in the daytime: the night will find them utterly unprepared for the judgment that they have so richly deserved.

As these teachers of error mingle among the people of God, they are spots and blemishes, marring and disturbing the fellowship of the saints, giving themselves over to self-indulgence as they feast with Christians as though they belonged to the family of God. Because there is no power in error to subdue nature's sinful lusts, these false teachers are described as having eyes full of adultery; they cannot cease from sin. It is only the might of the Holy Spirit that can subdue and hold in check the lusts of the flesh. False doctrines never do this. While beguiling or leading astray unstable souls—that is, those who are not well-grounded in the truth of God—they prove themselves to be an accursed generation whose hearts are exercised not unto godliness but with covetous practices.

Verse 15 tells us that having forsaken the right way they have gone astray, following the way of Balaam, the son of Bosor, who loved the wages of unrighteousness. While pretending to be subject to the Lord, Balaam craved the riches that Balak offered him if he could curse Israel for him. As Balaam hastened on his way, lured by the desire of gain, even the beast on which he rode rebuked him, as it beheld an angel of God in the way who sought to turn back the covetous prophet from his path. Men may ridicule and sneer at the idea of an ass speaking with a man's voice, but he who knows the Lord will remember that with God all things are possible.

While the propagators of unholy and unscriptural theories profess to have just the message that men need, they actually have nothing that can give victory over sin or relief to a troubled conscience. They are like wells without water that only disappoint the thirsty who go to them, or like clouds that look as though they might soon pour down refreshing showers but are carried away by gales of wind, and so the land is left as dry and arid as ever. The doom of these misleading teachers is sure. The mist of darkness is to be their portion forever. The sad thing is that, even among professing Christians, so many are ready to listen to these pretentious vendors of false systems only to be destroyed at last when they find that they are left without anything upon which the heart and conscience can rest for eternity.

Turning Away from the Truth to the False Philosophies of the World

For when they speak great swelling words of vanity, they allure through the lusts of the flesh, through much wantonness, those that were clean escaped from them who live in error. While they promise them liberty, they themselves are the servants of corruption: for of whom a man is overcome, of the same is he brought in bondage. For if after they have escaped the pollutions of the world through the knowledge of the Lord and Savior Jesus Christ, they are again entangled therein, and overcome, the latter end is worse with them than the beginning. For it had been better for them not to have known the way of righteousness, than, after they have known it, to turn from the holy commandment delivered unto them. But it is happened unto them according to the true proverb, The dog is turned to his own vomit again; and the sow that was washed to her wallowing in the mire. (vv. 18–22)

It is one thing to accept Christianity as a system; it is quite another to know Christ as Savior and Lord. Of all who are truly born again it can be said that "greater is he that is in you, than he that is in the world" (1 John 4:4). These are kept from error as they go on in dependence upon the Word of God as it is opened up to them by the Holy Spirit. But those who have merely taken up with a system of doctrines, however sound, are always in danger of giving them up for some other system and so becoming apostates, ensnared by the vainglorious language of false teachers who allure through the lusts of the flesh by presenting doctrines that appeal to hearts already turned wanton. Those who at one time had seemingly been completely delivered from sin and its folly are easily misled, and made to think that they are taking up with something superior to that which they already possess. But while these teachers promise their dupes liberty, they themselves are slaves of corruption because they know nothing of the liberty of grace, but rather are given to license instead. Overcome by sin they are brought into bondage.

Verses 20 and 21 have been taken by some as teaching that after people have been truly born again they are in danger of ceasing to be children of God and becoming once more the seed of Satan. It is well to observe that the Spirit of God is not contemplating reality here but simply profession. He speaks of those who have escaped the pollutions of the world through the knowledge of the Lord and Savior Jesus Christ, that is, having accepted the doctrines of Christianity. they have professedly given up the world, its sins and its folly, but there has never been a new nature imparted. They have not been born of God. Consequently, there is always the desire to gratify the lusts of the flesh, and when they come in contact with these false teachings they are easily entangled therewith and overcome, and so their latter end is worse with them than the beginning: that is, having given up the profession of Christianity and taken up with some false and unholy system of teaching, they throw off all restraint as to their lusts and live even more vilely than they did before they made a profession of conversion. Of these Peter says, "It had been better for them not to have known the way of righteousness, than, after they have known it, to turn from the holy commandment delivered unto them." Anyone who becomes acquainted with the teachings of Christianity knows the way of righteousness. Men who do not actually know Christ for themselves may give adherence to that way for the time being. Of those who have thus apostatized we read, "It is happened unto them according to the true proverb, The dog is turned to his own vomit again; and the sow that was washed to her wallowing in the mire." Charles H. Spurgeon well said on one occasion, "If that dog or that sow had been born again and had received the nature of a sheep it never would have gone back to the filth here depicted." The dog is used as a symbol of false teachers on more than one occasion in Scripture.

The sow is the natural man who may be cleansed outwardly but still loves the hog-wallow, and as soon as restraint is off he will go back to the filth in which he once lived.

CHAPTER 3

LOOKING ON TO
THE CULMINATION

2 Peter 3

A s Peter looked forward to the day when he should seal his own testimony
for Christ by laying down his life, as the Lord had foretold, he was the more
anxious to arouse the saints generally to the importance of maintaining their
confidence in what God had revealed concerning the prophetic future, or as we
say, "the last things." He had already reminded those to whom he wrote that
prophecy is a lamp to lighten the pilgrim along the dark road as he pursues his
way through this world to the Canaan rest, which will be his at the end of the
journey.

Now Peter stresses the importance of keeping the testimony of the prophets
and apostles in mind, when many will spurn them entirely.

Forgetting the Past and Denying the Future

This second epistle, beloved, I now write unto you; in both which I stir up your pure minds by way of remembrance: that ye may be mindful of the words which were spoken before by the holy prophets, and of the commandment of us the apostles of the Lord and Savior: knowing this first, that there shall come in the last days scoffers, walking after their own lusts, and saying, Where is the promise of his coming? for since the fathers fell asleep, all things continue as they were from the beginning of the creation. For this they willingly are ignorant of, that by the word of God the heavens were of old, and the earth standing out of the water and in the water: whereby the world that then was, being overflowed with water, perished: but the heavens and the earth, which are now, by the same word are kept in store, reserved unto fire against the day of judgment and perdition of ungodly men. (vv. 1–7)

In writing this second letter, guided by the Spirit of God, Peter was not endeavoring so much to open up new vistas of truth as to stir up the minds of the saints to the tremendous importance of keeping in memory what they had learned already. The words that were spoken in Old Testament times by the holy prophets, and the additional revelations communicated through the apostles of the new dispensation, should never be forgotten. Peter himself wrote as one of the latter group, having been definitely commissioned as an apostle by the Lord Jesus, and recognized by his brethren as being peculiarly adapted to make known the gospel to the Jews. When Paul tells us in the epistle to the Galatians that the brethren at Jerusalem acknowledged that the gospel of the uncircumcision had been committed to him as that of the circumcision had been committed to Peter (Gal. 2:7), we are not to suppose that he meant thereby that there was any fundamental difference in the messages themselves. It was rather that God had fitted Paul in a very definite way to carry the gospel to the Gentiles; whereas Peter was more adapted to minister the Word of grace to the Jews. As a result of his ministry, many of the dispersion had been brought to know the Lord. And in obedience to the command given Peter on the shore of the Sea of Galilee he undertook to feed these sheep and lambs of Christ's flock both by word of mouth and in these epistles. He puts before them, therefore, in the strongest possible way the necessity of keeping in mind the Holy Scriptures of the Old and the New Testaments. The Old Testament had been complete for centuries, but the New Testament was not yet complete. Nevertheless many of its books were in circulation already, and among them were all the epistles of Paul, as we shall see later in considering the closing verses of this same chapter. Recognizing in these books the testimony of God Himself, who by the Holy Spirit had inspired the human authorship of each portion of the Word, Peter urges the saints not to neglect the Scriptures but ever keep them in their hearts, in order that they may shed light not only on the present pathway but also on the future to which they were hastening. It had been predicted again and again by both prophets and apostles that in the last days there would be those who would utterly repudiate the truth of a divine revelation as to the return of the Lord. These scoffers would hate the truth because it interfered with their own selfish desires, and they would sneer at the very possibility of the second advent of the Savior.

That of which Peter spoke as being in the future and as that which would be manifested in the last days we now see fully developed all around us. Everywhere we find men walking after their own ungodly lusts, deriding the doctrine of the imminent return of the Lord as though it were something utterly ridiculous and not to be considered for a moment by sober-minded people. Even in the pulpits of many professedly orthodox churches ministers today take this stand, either denying that the Bible itself teaches the second coming of Christ, or else maintaining that even though predicted by Christ and taught by His apostles, it is all to be looked upon as an idle dream. These men ask contemptuously, "Where is the promise of His coming?" They declare that "since the fathers fell asleep, all things continue as they were from the beginning of the creation"—that is, they insist that there is no evidence whatever in the history of the past or in conditions prevailing at the present time that indicate the fulfillment of any prophetic declarations. Though wise as to the things of this world, they are absolutely ignorant of the signs of the times—signs that spiritually-minded and godly men discern readily, but that these carnal and sensual leaders of religious thought ignore completely. As in the days before the flood the men of Noah's day refused to give credence to the testimony of the Lord in regard to a coming judgment and knew not until the flood came and took them all away, so will it be with many in this generation who contemptuously discard all that Scripture teaches in regard to the coming day of the Lord, while all the time the world is rushing forward into the fearful vortex of that day of wrath.

Many have forgotten that "by the Word of God the heavens were of old, and the earth standing out of the water and in the water: whereby the world that then was, being overflowed with water, perished." The men who lived in antediluvian times said unto God, "Depart from us; for we desire not the knowledge of thy ways" (Job 21:14). As Eliphaz reminded Job when he said, "Hast thou marked the old way which wicked men have trodden? which were cut down out of time, whose foundation was overflown with a flood: which said unto God, Depart from us: and what can the Almighty do for them? Yet he filled their houses with good things: but the counsel of the wicked is far from me" (Job 22:15–18). So it will be with many in this age. They are willingly ignorant of God's dealings with men in the past, and therefore refuse to believe in any predictions of judgments to come.

There is something very striking in the expression, "Kept in store, reserved unto fire." The passage might be translated "the heavens and the earth are stored with fire, awaiting the day of judgment and perdition of ungodly men." We might have some conception of what this means as we think of the fearful catastrophe produced by the atomic bomb, which was, even to those who discovered it, a terrible revelation of the powers for destruction that are reserved in the heavens. When earth's long day has run its course there will come not another flood but a universal conflagration, which will sweep this globe clean of all that men have built up during the millennia of the past, and prepare for a new heaven and a new earth wherein dwelleth righteousness.

The Day of the Lord and the Day of God

But, beloved, be not ignorant of this one thing, that one day is with the Lord as a thousand years, and a thousand years as one day. The Lord is not slack concerning his promise, as some men count slackness; but is longsuffering to us-ward, not willing that any should perish, but that all should come to repentance. But the day of the Lord will come as a thief in the night; in the which the heavens shall pass away with a great noise, and the elements shall melt with fervent heat, the earth also and the works that are therein shall be burned up. Seeing then that all these things shall be dissolved, what manner of persons ought ye to be in all holy conversation and godliness, looking for and hasting unto the coming of the day of God, wherein the heavens being on fire shall be dissolved, and the elements shall melt with fervent heat? Nevertheless we, according to his promise, look for new heavens and a new earth, wherein dwelleth righteousness. Wherefore, beloved, seeing that ye look for such things, be diligent that ye may be found of him in peace, without spot, and blameless. (vv. 8–14)

Because these willfully ignorant men do not see the evidences of this, they deny what they do not understand, and, "Because sentence against an evil work is not executed speedily, therefore the heart of the sons of men is fully set in them to do evil," as we are told in the book of Ecclesiastes (8:11). If judgment seems to tarry it is not because God has forgotten, but rather because of His deep concern about lost men whom, in His loving-kindness, He still desires to save. Our thoughts are not His thoughts, neither are our ways His ways, but as the heavens are higher than the earth, so are His ways above our ways, and His thoughts above our thoughts (Isa. 55:8). A thousand years may seem a long time to men, whose span of life very seldom reaches a century, but one day is with the Lord as a thousand years, and a thousand years as one day. Not two days have passed, therefore, according to the divine reckoning, since the Lord Jesus went away after giving the promise, "I will come again" (John 14:3). It is not, then, that the Lord is slack regarding His promise, as men are disposed to think, but His heart still goes out to those who are persisting in rebellion against Him; and He waits in grace, still proclaiming the gospel message and offering salvation to all who turn to Him in repentance, because He is not willing that any should perish.

But when at last the day of grace is ended, the day of the Lord will succeed it, and that day will come to unbelievers as a thief in the night. The day of the Lord is not to be confounded with the day of Christ, which refers to the return of the Lord in the air to call His saints to be with Him, when they will appear before His judgment seat to be rewarded according to the measure of their faithfulness to Him while they have been pilgrims here below. The day of the Lord follows that. It will be the time when the judgments of God are being poured out upon the earth. It includes the descent of the Lord with all His saints to execute judgment on His foes, and to take possession of the kingdom so long predicted, and to reign in righteousness for a thousand glorious years in this very world where He once was crucified. As that great day of the Lord closes, the heavens and the earth shall pass away with a great noise, and the elements shall melt with fervent heat.

This last expression is far easier understood today than it ever has been in past centuries because of recent discoveries in connection with the explosive power of certain elements, such as uranium, when brought under terrific pressure. Following the destruction of the created heavens and this lower universe as we now know them, will come the fulfillment of the prediction of Isaiah (65:17) concerning a new heaven and a new earth wherein righteousness will dwell forever. This eternal condition is the day of God, in view of which the present created heavens and earth will be destroyed. The day of God is unending; it includes all the ages to come when sin will be forever banished from the universe, and righteousness will be everywhere manifest. Righteousness suffers during the present age. Those who would walk in obedience to the Word of God often are persecuted by those who seek to maintain the present order of things.

In the millennium, righteousness will reign: the authority of the Lord Jesus will be everywhere established, and evil will be held down; but in the eternal state, righteousness will dwell, for all evil will have been banished to the lake of fire.

A Final Warning

> And account that the longsuffering of our Lord is salvation; even as our beloved brother Paul also according to the wisdom given unto him hath written unto you; as also in all his epistles, speaking in them of these things; in which are some things hard to be understood, which they that are unlearned and unstable wrest, as they do also the other scriptures, unto their own destruction. Ye therefore, beloved, seeing ye know these things before, beware lest ye also, being led away with the error of the wicked, fall from your own steadfastness. But grow in grace, and in the knowledge of our Lord and Savior Jesus Christ. To him be glory both now and for ever. Amen. (vv. 15–18)

So then God's patience and long-suffering with mankind throughout all the centuries of human history are ever with a view to the salvation of any who will turn to Him, confessing their sin and believing the message of His grace.

Peter adds, "Even as our beloved brother Paul also according to the wisdom given unto him hath written unto you." This is very clearly an authentication of the Pauline authorship of the epistle to the Hebrews. There can be no other writing to which he refers in this verse. As we have seen, Peter himself was addressing converted Jews or Hebrews. He tells us that the apostle Paul had written a letter to the same people. There is no other of Paul's letters addressed to converted Jews but the epistle to the Hebrews. And in that epistle to the Hebrews Paul corroborates the testimony of Peter in regard to these eschatological truths, which he has just been unfolding. In Hebrews 12:25–29 we get this corroborative testimony: "See that ye refuse not him that speaketh. For if they escaped not who refused him that spake on earth, much more shall not we escape, if we turn away from him that speaketh from heaven: whose voice then shook the earth: but now he hath promised, saying, Yet once more I shake not the earth only, but also heaven. And this word, Yet once more, signifieth the removing of those things that are shaken, as of things that are made, that those things which cannot be shaken may remain. Wherefore we receiving a kingdom which cannot be moved, let us have grace, whereby we may serve God acceptably with reverence and godly fear: for our God is a consuming fire." Here we have set forth exactly the same truths that the apostle Peter has been stressing. There should be no question, therefore, but that Peter was declaring that Paul was the author of this particular epistle.

Then Peter goes on to say that in this special letter to the Hebrews, as also in all his epistles, Paul had spoken of these things; and in these letters there are "some things hard to be understood, which they that are unlearned and unstable wrest, as they do also the other scriptures, unto their own destruction." In this way Peter acknowledges Paul's letters to be accepted by all believers as the very Word of God. There are, in the epistle to the Hebrews particularly, a number of passages that have caused untold distress to those who have but a feeble understanding of God's great plan. Take such passages, for instance, as Hebrews 6:4–8 and 10:26–31. How often has the Devil used these Scriptures to trouble unstable souls with the awful thought that perhaps they have committed some unpardonable sin and so are hopelessly beyond the reach of mercy! While the passages themselves suggest nothing of the kind, yet they have been used of the Enemy to disturb many. In others of Paul's writings there are passages that have been misused in the same way, but more notable in Hebrews than in any other epistle.

Peter closes with two admonitions. In verse 17 he says, "Ye therefore, beloved, seeing ye know these things before, beware lest ye also, being led away with the error of the wicked, fall from your own steadfastness." No one will ever thus fail who keeps his eyes on Christ and his heart fixed on those things that are above where Christ sits at God's right hand. Doctrinal error of a serious character is almost invariably connected with some moral failure. As we walk before God in holiness of life we will be preserved from destructive heresies, and as we walk in the truth we will be kept from sin in the life.

The final admonition is found in the last verse: "Grow in grace, and in the knowledge of our Lord and Savior Jesus Christ." This is the unfailing panacea for all spiritual ills. As we go on to know Christ better and become increasingly like Him, and as we feed upon His Word, and it has its sway over our hearts, our progress will be consistent and continuous.

The final doxology is a very brief but a very precious one: "To him be glory both now and for ever. Amen." How Peter's own heart must have been moved as he wrote these words! He had known Christ intimately in the days of His flesh; he himself had failed so grievously on the night of the betrayal; he had been restored so blessedly, both secretly and publicly, by the Lord Himself: so that Christ had become the all-absorbing passion of his soul. Christ alone deserved all the praise and all the glory, and that to the age of ages—the uttermost limits of that day of God, the day of eternity of which we have been reading.